Substance Abuse

The Nation's Number One Health Problem

Key Indicators for Policy **Update**

February 2001

Prepared by the Schneider Institute for Health Policy, Brandeis University
for The Robert Wood Johnson Foundation, Princeton, New Jersey

Principal Investigator
Constance Horgan

Lead Investigator for Overview and Section I
Kathleen Carley Skwara

Lead Investigator for Sections II and III
Gail Strickler

Chart Coordinator
Lisa Andersen

Editor
Jane J. Stein, The Stein Group

The Robert Wood Johnson Foundation (RWJF)
Project Director
Joan Hollendonner

RWJF Editorial and Production Staff
C. Tracy Orleans, Nancy Kaufman,
Frank Karel, Joan Barlow, Jeanne Weber,
Hope Woodhead, Edna Bijou and
RWJF consultant Senta German

Book and Chart Design
DBA Design

Schneider Institute for Health Policy
Heller Graduate School
Brandeis University
415 South Street, MS 035
Waltham, MA 02454–9110
http://ihp.brandeis.edu

The Robert Wood Johnson Foundation
Route 1 and College Road East
P.O. Box 2316
Princeton, NJ 08543–2316
www.rwjf.org

ISBN 0–942054–13–X
February 2001

Table of Contents

Table of Contents (continued)

Acknowledgements

We would like to thank a number of people who provided very helpful advice on aspects of this report, including the content and locating data sources. We are grateful to the Co-Principal Investigators for the 1993 version of the chartbook, Mary Ellen Marsden and Mary Jo Larson, who reviewed this update. Other Brandeis staff contributing to the chartbook were John Capitman, Corinne Kay, Brad Krevor, Sharon Reif, Mark Sciegaj, Linda Simoni-Wastila and Elizabeth Tighe.

Many individuals from The Robert Wood Johnson Foundation, especially Joan Hollendonner, C. Tracy Orleans and Nancy Kaufman, provided useful advice and comments. Other reviewers at the Foundation were Elize Brown, Jack Ebeler, Seth Emont, Robert Hughes, Paul Jellinek, J. Michael McGinnis, Constance Pechura and Steven Schroeder. External reviewers included Marilyn Aguirre-Molina, Dianne Barker, Carl Leukefeld, Lorraine Midanik, James Neal and Sharyn Sutton. Dorothy Rice and Rick Harwood provided special cost calculations. Researchers at the University of Michigan provided unpublished data from the annual Monitoring the Future Survey. Also helpful were Michael Cummings, Joseph Gfroerer and Gary Giovino.

Constance Horgan, Kathleen Carley Skwara and Gail Strickler

Preface

The mission of The Robert Wood Johnson Foundation is to improve the health and health care of all Americans. Substance abuse causes more deaths, illnesses and disabilities than any other preventable health condition, and it affects Americans from all walks of life. It is fitting then that one of our three grant-making priorities is to promote health and reduce the personal, social and economic harm caused by substance abuse—tobacco, alcohol and illicit drugs.

As a national philanthropy, the Foundation uses a variety of strategies in pursuing this goal. These include support for innovative institutions that bring the best resources to bear on the problem; projects to increase public interest and support for solutions; community-based service and demonstration projects; integrating the most effective prevention and treatment strategies into medical and other systems; career development; and creation and dissemination of new knowledge.

Because everyone has a role to play in addressing substance abuse, this second edition of *Substance Abuse: The Nation's Number One Health Problem* has been designed with a broad and diverse audience in mind—educators, prevention and treatment practitioners, policymakers, researchers, the media and others. The book presents key policy-relevant indicators with an emphasis on trends over time. We call this "data for action," because a knowledgeable public is in a better position to make decisions and take action. Following an overview, the book is divided into three parts and is designed to provide building blocks of information. Beginning with patterns of use, it moves on to the consequences of use and concludes with ways to combat the problem.

While trend data show that tobacco, alcohol and other drug use are down from the peak levels of earlier decades, and the perception of risk associated with substance abuse has increased since then, pockets of high use remain, and risky experimentation by youth continues. Much remains to be done. As President and CEO of the Foundation, and a practicing physician who witnesses the ravages of substance abuse on patients' health, I hope the information provided in this book will help show the way to a better understanding of the nation's number one health problem and ways that we can deal with it.

Steven A. Schroeder, MD
President and CEO
The Robert Wood Johnson Foundation

Data Notes

About the terms used in this report

The labels used in this report for population groups, risk groups and health problems are those used by the original data sources. For instance, sometimes we use the word drugs; other times we use illicit drugs. In some cases, these labels—ethnic and racial identities are an example—reflect old values. We adopted this approach, despite our desire to be sensitive to changing preferences, because of the lack of consensus about which terms are preferred and to avoid potential confusion when people go back to an original data source to learn more about an issue.

Cautionary notes for data interpretation

This report presents data on trends in substance use, consequences and intervention efforts, as well as comparisons among subgroups of the population on these issues. When appropriate, numbers were rounded to the nearest whole number. In most cases, available information was not sufficient to test for statistical significance of differences between years or between subgroups. Accordingly, caution should be exercised in comparing the magnitude of such differences.

Trend data generally are drawn from cross-sectional surveys or other data that do not represent the experience of the same individuals over time. In addition, these data represent the years in which surveys were conducted, and lags or blanks in the data reflect years in which surveys were not conducted. For example, the National Household Survey on Drug Abuse has been conducted annually only since 1990; prior to that it was conducted less frequently. When the data span a period of years, we show the changes within those years when the data are available, even when we do not list the data in the table below the indicator.

We have included two indicators in the appendices that chart our nation's progress on the *Healthy People 2000* objectives for tobacco, alcohol and other drugs. These two indicators use data from the National Center for Health Statistic's *Healthy People 2000 Review*, 1998-1999. In some instances, information in the text may reflect more recent data than is shown in the appendices.

Despite these cautionary notes, the consistency of long-term trends and evidence from several sources is supportive of the major conclusions about the magnitude of the substance abuse problem and the progress made in combating it.

Overview: The Context of Substance Abuse

The abuse of alcohol, tobacco and illicit drugs places an enormous burden on the country. As the nation's number one health problem, it strains the health care system and contributes to the death and ill health of millions of Americans every year and to the high cost of health care. Substance abuse—the problematic use of alcohol, tobacco and illicit drugs—also harms family life, the economy and public safety. It gives many of our children and youth a poor start in life. Although all segments of society are involved, it disproportionately affects disadvantaged groups.

Billions of dollars are spent by the federal government to control substance abuse, with some promising results:

- *Overall, rates of current illicit drug and alcohol use are down from peak levels in the late 1970s and early 1980s, respectively, and current tobacco use has declined since the mid-1960s.*
- *Public awareness about the dangers of substance abuse is up.*
- *Prevention and treatment strategies are increasingly effective when applied to reduce substance abuse and its effects on the nation.*

As we begin a new century, many problems relating to substance abuse need to be solved. Illicit drugs are still widely available, and tobacco and alcohol continue to be easily accessible to underage youth; rates of use and experimentation by youth are on the rise for some substances; and while there are effective prevention and treatment programs, they are underused and not broadly available.

A Health and Social Problem

There are more deaths, illnesses and disabilities from substance abuse than from any other preventable health condition. Of the more than two million deaths each year in the United States, approximately one in four is attributable to alcohol, tobacco and illicit drug use, with tobacco causing about 430,700 deaths, followed by more than 100,000 for alcohol and nearly 16,000 for illicit drugs. Smoking—whether it is active or passive—causes myriad adverse health effects, including cardiovascular disease, cancers and respiratory problems in children and adults. Many of these premature deaths and health problems could be reduced—if not eliminated—by changing behaviors. Treatment of medical problems caused by substance use and abuse places a huge burden on the health care system.

Alcohol and illicit drug use can result in family violence and mistreatment of children, and the death of a family member due to substance abuse has lasting ramifications. The workplace is affected, as well. Alcohol and drug abusers are less productive employees.

Annually, millions of people are arrested for driving under the influence of alcohol or illicit drugs and other offenses related to alcohol and drug use. The safety of many neighborhoods—and the people living and working in them—is threatened by the violence associated with drug sales. Federal, state and local governments, as well as private citizens' groups, have acted to counter the enormous societal impact of substance abuse, but much remains to be done.

This report describes the magnitude of the substance abuse problem. It presents indicators that describe the nature and extent of substance use and abuse; associated consequences; and efforts to combat the problems related to use, abuse and dependency. Descriptive findings are provided throughout, including measures that document changes over time. Changes in these indicators will help determine successful efforts and where additional resources need to be targeted.

Use, Abuse and Dependence

Many people who drink, smoke or take illicit drugs may not develop a physical dependency or have negative experiences from using these substances (although it is possible to have a serious injury or even die from a single episode of alcohol or drug use). However, heavier, longer-term and more frequent consumption, associated with addictive use patterns, is likely to result in problems with health, family members and other people, school, work or the law.

Substance abuse involves patterns of increasing levels of use that result in health consequences or impairment in social, psychological and/or occupational functioning. Addiction is a chronic, relapsing brain disease. Substance dependence or addiction involves compulsive use and is usually accompanied by craving, increased tolerance and substantial impairment of health and social functioning. A person who is dependent on a substance needs it—often in increasing amounts—even when trying to cut back. Great progress is being made in understanding how the behavioral and psychosocial aspects of addiction are triggered by drug-induced changes in the brain.

Although it is not possible to predict who will develop problems with substances and under what circumstances, in general, more serious problems develop when people become dependent on alcohol, tobacco and illicit drugs. The process of becoming dependent is complex and is related to a number of factors, including the addictive properties of the substance, family and peer influences, personality, cultural and social factors and existing psychiatric disorders.

Genetics also plays a recognized role in explaining individual susceptibility to substance abuse and addiction and initial responses to alcohol, tobacco and illicit drugs, with new findings emerging rapidly. In addition, research suggests that substance use in the pre-adolescent and early adolescent years increases the likelihood of later substance dependence. The scientific evidence is clear: alcohol, tobacco and illicit drugs are addictive substances.

Substance dependence is often described as a chronic, relapsing condition characterized by waves of abuse, decreased use and abuse again. It is difficult to quit or curtail use, and for many, more than one attempt is needed—sometimes over a long period of time—before a person successfully quits or gets use under control.

Historical Trends in Consumption and Policy

The use of alcohol, tobacco and illicit drugs has fluctuated during this century in response to shifts in public tolerance and with various political, economic and social events. Overall, smoking began to decrease in the mid-1960s, drug use in the late 1970s and alcohol consumption in the early 1980s. Many people attribute these decreases to:

- increased awareness of the health risks;
- government involvement in prevention, intervention and treatment efforts;
- environmental policy changes, such as workplace bans on smoking; and
- the development of grassroots efforts and community coalitions directed toward decreasing substance abuse.

However, tobacco and illicit drug use increased among youth between the early 1990s and 1996. These increases may have been related to several factors occurring during that time, such as: a decreasing perception of potential harm from use, especially marijuana; the decline in the prevalence of anti-drug messages and warnings from parents, the media and school; pro-use messages from the entertainment industry; increased marketing by the tobacco industry; and increases in cigarette smoking, which may be associated with the increased use of other drugs. There are signs that trends in use may be shifting downward, with recent declines in the use of most illicit drugs for 8th, 10th and 12th graders since the mid-1990s.

Alcohol

Alcohol consumption in the United States has risen and fallen over time. It was high during the Civil War, World War I and World War II and low during Prohibition (the 1919 constitutional amendment prohibiting the manufacture, transportation and sale of alcohol, which was repealed in 1933) and the Depression (Indicator 1). Consumption was the lowest in U.S. history—0.97 gallons of ethanol per person age 15 and older—in 1934, when the Depression was at its peak, and highest at 2.8 gallons per capita (per person age 14 and older) around 1980, following a period during which more than half the states lowered the legal drinking age to 18. In 1997, per capita consumption of ethanol was 2.18 gallons—with beer consumption at 1.24 gallons of ethanol, spirits at 0.63 gallons and wine at 0.31 gallons.

Since the early 1980s, alcohol consumption has declined generally with the exception of several slight increases in the 1990s. This overall decline coincided with raising the minimum drinking age to 21 in all states to counter the alarming number of fatal automobile crashes involving teenagers and alcohol. The decrease is also due to a decline in the consumption of distilled spirits starting around 1980. Beer consumption also declined slightly. These overall trends in current alcohol consumption mask many important differences in drinking patterns during one's lifetime and among demographic groups, as described in this report.

Alcohol is the most commonly used drug among young people, and there may be serious implications from this early use. Rates of use are still high, with 50 percent of high school seniors reporting drinking in the past 30 days and 32 percent reporting being drunk at least once in this same time frame. Moreover, widespread binge drinking among college students has been called the most serious public health problem on college campuses.

As a result, there is an emerging research focus on strategies to reduce underage alcohol use. These strategies include limitations on access and availability of alcohol to minors, expressions of community norms against underage alcohol use, prevention of impaired driving, school-based programs and comprehensive approaches. Other public policies have focused on marketing control policies (e.g., restrictions on alcohol sponsorship at community events), policies that control distribution (e.g., keg registration and regulations regarding home delivery of alcohol), regulation of outlets that serve alcohol and additional policies regarding sellers.

Indicator 1

Trends in Alcohol Use, 1850–1997

Annual per Capita Consumption in Gallons of Ethanol

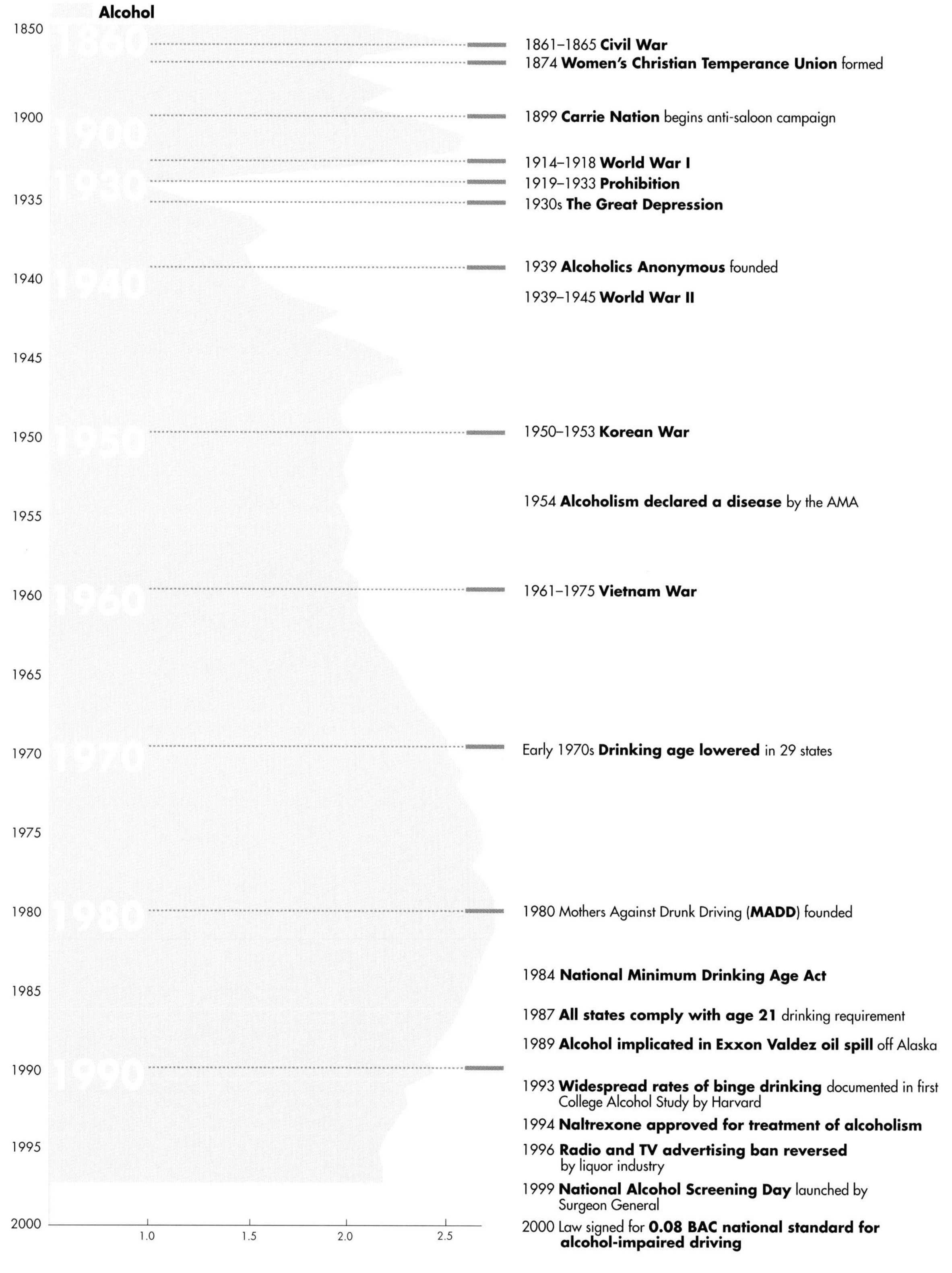

NOTES: Alcohol consumption is measured by converting the gallons of sold or shipped wine, beer and spirits into gallons of ethanol (pure alcohol), using estimates of average ethanol content for each beverage type. Per capita estimates are then calculated per person age 15 and older prior to 1970 and per person age 14 and older thereafter.

SOURCE: National Institute on Alcohol Abuse and Alcoholism, Division of Biometry and Epidemiology. *Apparent Per Capita Alcohol Consumption: National, State, and Regional Trends, 1977–1997.* Surveillance Report No. 51. December 1999. Table 1, p.16.

Alcohol remains the number one drug of choice among both adolescents and adults and is the most widely available drug. Rates of dependency associated with alcohol use are higher than those for illicit drugs. Consequently, alcohol is listed most often as the primary drug of abuse among those in substance abuse treatment. Further, the economic cost of alcohol abuse exceeds that of either tobacco or illicit drugs.

Tobacco

Tobacco is a part of our earliest history, predating the arrival of Columbus. American Indians had long cultivated tobacco and used it for religious purposes in various forms, including cigars, cigarettes, chewing tobacco and pipes. During the 17th century, tobacco became an important cash crop for North Carolina, and by 1864 it was a significant enough commodity that a federal tax was imposed on cigarettes to help finance the Civil War. By the 1890s, machines were perfected that produced cigarettes in much greater volume than was possible with hand rolling.

Cigarette consumption increased dramatically between 1900 and the mid-1960s, with peaks and valleys paralleling historical events. It was slightly higher during World War I and World War II, and lower during the Depression years (Indicator 2). Annual consumption peaked in 1963, at 4,345 cigarettes per person age 18 and older per year. (Smoking a pack of cigarettes a day amounts to about 7,500 cigarettes a year.) The precipitating event for the decline since then was the 1964 Surgeon General's report that definitively linked cigarette smoking to health problems.

Over the years, the tobacco industry has introduced a number of marketing and product design strategies to curb or reverse downward trends or anticipated declines in tobacco consumption. Through the development of new products, the tobacco industry has tried to attract new smokers and keep current smokers from quitting. For example, filter cigarettes were promoted heavily during the 1950s, low-tar cigarettes were introduced in the 1960s, chewing or spit tobacco was redesigned and reintroduced as an alternative to smoking in the 1970s and smokeless and perfumed cigarettes were introduced in the 1980s. More recently, the tobacco industry has engaged in targeted marketing techniques, including ads aimed at minorities and women, promotional gear marketed to youth and so-called smokeless or spit tobacco to attract young men. Finally, tobacco companies decreased prices to counter state tobacco excise tax increases.

Indicator 2

Trends in Cigarette Use, 1900–2000

Annual per Capita Consumption of Cigarettes for Those 18 Years and Over

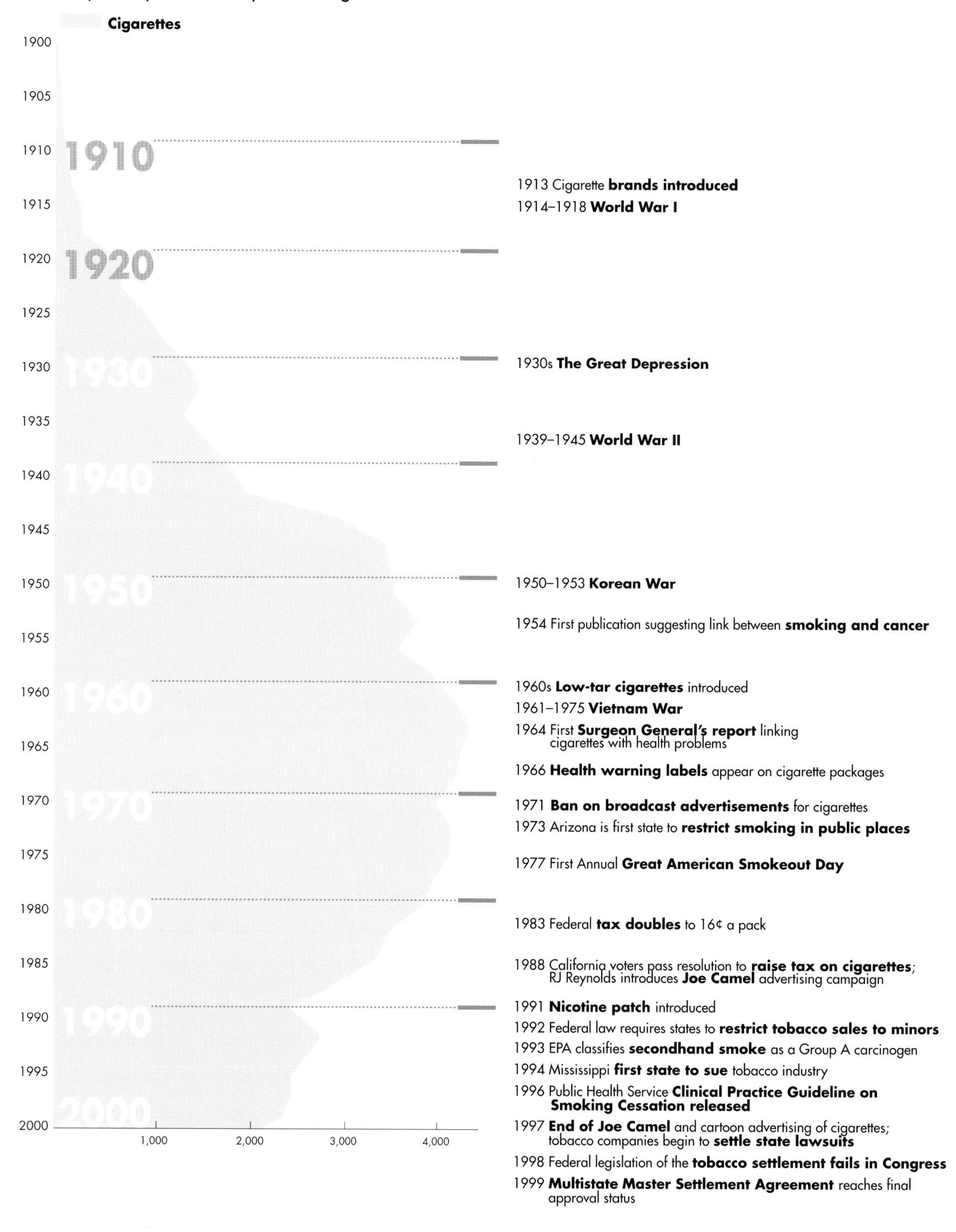

NOTE: Data for 2000 are preliminary.

SOURCES: For 1900–1974: *Tobacco Yearbook, 1981*. Col. Clem Cockrel. Bowling Green, KY, p. 53. For 1975–1981: U.S. Department of Agriculture. *Tobacco Situation and Outlook Report.* Rockville, MD: Commodity Economics Division, Economic Research Service, 1985. Table 2, p. 6. For 1982–1989: U.S. Department of Agriculture. *Tobacco Situation and Outlook Report.* Rockville, MD: Commodity Economics Division, Economic Research Service, 1992. Table 2, p. 4. For 1990–1999: U.S. Department of Agriculture. *Tobacco Situation and Outlook Report.* Washington, DC: Market and Trade Economics Division, Economic Research Service, 2000. Table 2. For 2000: U.S. Department of Agriculture. *Tobacco Situation and Outlook Report.* Washington, DC: Market and Trade Economics Division, Economic Research Service, September 2000. Table 2.

In spite of these efforts, cigarette consumption continues to decline, with the 2000 expected per capita consumption at its lowest since 1963—an estimated 2,054 cigarettes per person per year—roughly the same as in the early 1940s. The decreases have not been uniform across all groups, however. Historically, smoking rates were greater for males than females, but over time this gap has narrowed, with rates dropping more dramatically for men.

A study of 8th, 10th and 12th graders showed increases in smoking rates between the early 1990s and 1996, with substantial declines in recent years. Smoking among college students, however, increased between 1993 and 1997. Cigar use has also increased recently, with 6.9 percent of the overall population reporting past month use.

In recent years, government efforts to combat tobacco use have increased. In 1996, the Food and Drug Administration (FDA) issued regulations to further restrict the sale and distribution of cigarettes and smokeless tobacco products to minors. In 2000, the U.S. Supreme Court ruled that the FDA does not have the authority to regulate tobacco; this issue is expected to be the focus of a renewed congressional legislative effort. Four states—Mississippi, Florida, Texas and Minnesota—settled lawsuits filed against the tobacco industry seeking compensation for tobacco-related Medicaid costs. The remaining states and five territories became part of the landmark November 1998 settlement agreement with the tobacco industry known as the Multistate Master Settlement Agreement (MSA). The agreement, which settles all pending legal actions against the tobacco industry by the state attorneys general and requires the tobacco industry to pay $206 billion to the states, reached final approval status in November 1999.

Illicit drugs

The history of illicit drug use in the United States is marked by shifts in public attitudes and policies between tolerance and intolerance. During the late 1800s, laissez-faire approaches to drug use began to be supplanted by increasing government regulation as the medical profession and public became aware of the addictive properties of certain drugs. At that time, cocaine and opiates, which were inexpensive and readily available, were used widely in nonprescription products. A series of legislative acts and court cases during the first two decades of the 20th century resulted in a decrease in cocaine and opiate use, and the nation's drug problem diminished during the Depression and World War II.

During the 1950s and 1960s, however, heroin emerged as a problem in our cities, and use of a variety of illicit drugs grew among the general population in the 1970s, peaking later in the decade for most drugs. The 1960s and 1970s also saw the development of new treatment approaches, including methadone maintenance (long-term use of a synthetic narcotic to treat heroin addiction), residential programs, including therapeutic communities (drug treatment programs that stress values and personal growth) and outpatient care (ambulatory care at a hospital or facility).

In general, the use of any illicit drug decreased among most segments of the population during the 1980s and has remained fairly stable for those age 18 and older in the 1990s. However, there are varying patterns related to specific substances. Cocaine use peaked in the mid-1980s, and heroin use increased in the 1990s. Methamphetamine and hallucinogen use also increased in the 1990s.

Illicit drug use—particularly marijuana use—rose among youth in grades 8, 10 and 12 from the early 1990s to the mid-1990s, although rates have since declined from these recent peak levels. A notable exception is the recent sharp increase in ecstasy use among teens. In the 1990s, much of the increase in hallucinogen and heroin use was attributable to increases among those under age 26.

To illustrate recent trends, selected historical events are charted against past month marijuana and cocaine use among 18- to 25-year-olds from 1974 to 1998 (Indicator 3). This age group has high overall rates of illicit drug use, but especially marijuana and cocaine. By 1979, 36 percent of 18- to 25-year-olds reported past month marijuana use. This was a peak period, not only for marijuana use among 18- to 25-year-olds, but also for most drugs and for most age groups. Since then, marijuana use has generally decreased; in 1998, about 14 percent of 18- to 25-year-olds reported using marijuana in the past month. Cocaine use in this age group also peaked in 1979 at 10 percent in the past month, falling to 2 percent in 1998.

There is continued concern over the impact of illicit drug use. New research shows that even low doses of cocaine can cause constriction of blood vessels in the brain in otherwise healthy people. This research also suggests that cocaine can have a negative cumulative effect on brain function. The recent upswing in heroin use, as well as uncertain dosage levels, makes heroin, which is responsible for

Indicator 3

Trends in Illicit Drug Use, 1974–1998

Percent Past Month Marijuana and Cocaine Users among Those Ages 18–25

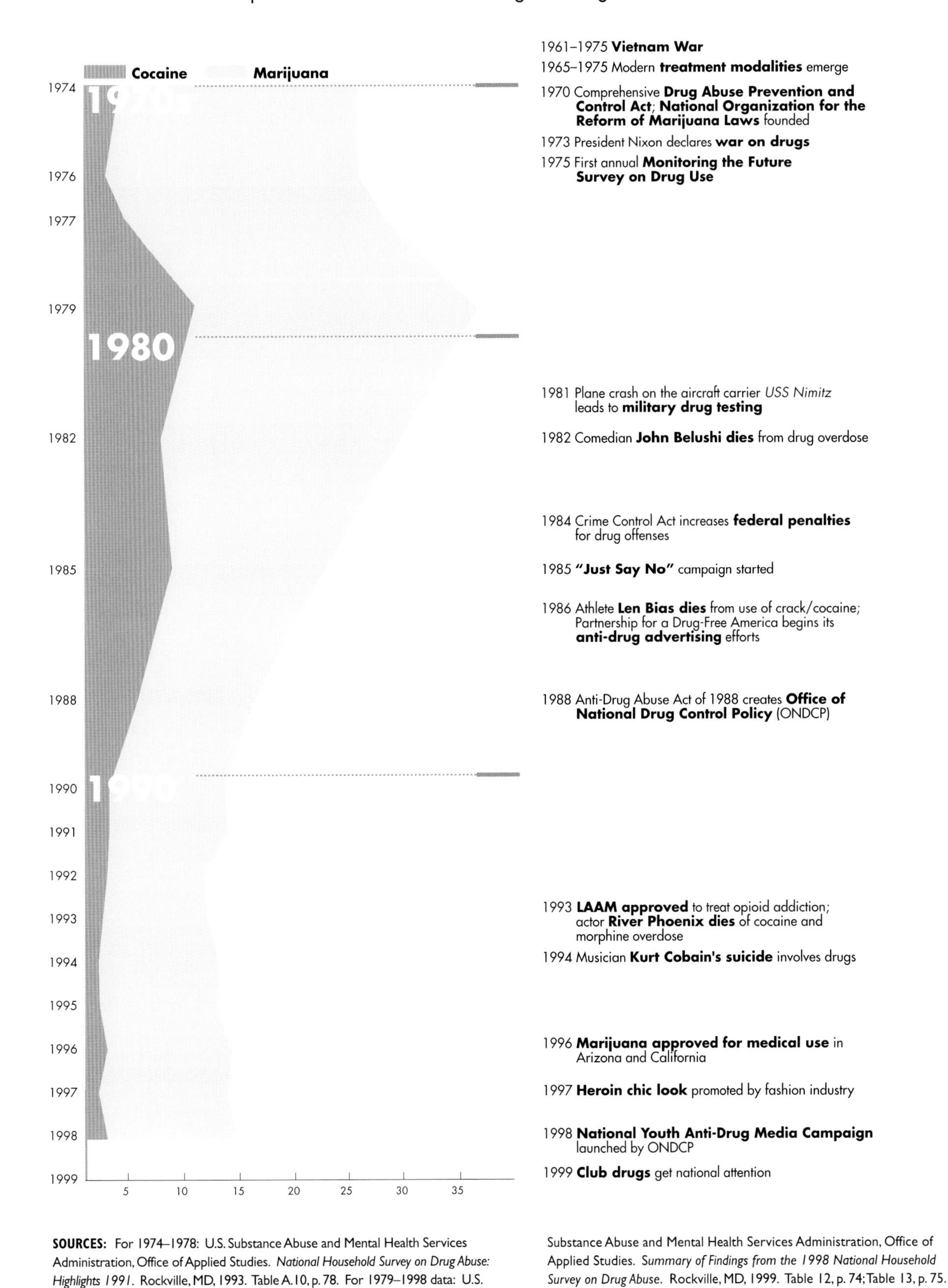

SOURCES: For 1974–1978: U.S. Substance Abuse and Mental Health Services Administration, Office of Applied Studies. *National Household Survey on Drug Abuse: Highlights 1991*. Rockville, MD, 1993. Table A.10, p. 78. For 1979–1998 data: U.S. Substance Abuse and Mental Health Services Administration, Office of Applied Studies. *Summary of Findings from the 1998 National Household Survey on Drug Abuse*. Rockville, MD, 1999. Table 12, p. 74; Table 13, p. 75.

more deaths than any other illicit drug, particularly dangerous. Some of the increase in new heroin users since 1992 may be explained in part by increased purity and different modes of transmission (smoking, snorting or sniffing), which may make the drug appealing to more users, especially young people.

Injecting drug users, their partners and offspring are now driving the HIV epidemic. Also, numerous studies have documented the relationship of illicit drug use to crime and violence.

All Segments of Society Affected

No population group is immune to substance abuse and its effects. Men and women, people of all ages, racial and ethnic groups and levels of education drink, smoke and use illicit drugs. In 1998, approximately 13.6 million Americans were current illicit drug users, and in 1997, 52 million smoked. Unlike with the use of tobacco and illicit drugs, there may be health benefits associated with moderate alcohol use for some, although even moderate levels of drinking are implicated in accidental injury and death. In 1998, nearly 113 million Americans had used alcohol in the past month. There are significant differences, however, in substance use among certain groups. Young adults, for example, are the group most likely to use alcohol, tobacco and illicit drugs, and many adolescents have already started. Men are more likely than women to use most substances, and they are particularly more likely to be heavy users of alcohol.

Whites are more likely than blacks or Hispanics to drink alcohol, and their rates of heavy alcohol use are higher than among blacks but lower than among Hispanics. American Indians and Alaskan Natives, meanwhile, are more apt to have problems with alcohol. Minorities are disproportionately represented among injecting drug users with AIDS. In 1998, 37 percent of non-Hispanic black males and 36 percent of Hispanic males with AIDS contracted HIV through injecting drug use, in contrast to only 13 percent of white males.

Level of education is increasingly recognized as an important correlate of substance use, with heavier use among those with less education. People with more education are more likely to drink, but those with less education are more likely to drink heavily. Among people with less education, smoking is more common, and smoking cessation less likely. Similarly, current illicit drug use is twice as high among those age 26 to 34 who have not completed high school than among those with a college degree.

It is also important to note that substance abuse problems cluster within subpopulations. These problems are more prevalent among the economically disadvantaged, including low-income, blue-collar and ethnic/racial minority groups. They also cluster in individuals. For instance, risky drinking, alcoholism and illicit drug use are more common among smokers than nonsmokers. This underscores the growing need for programs and treatments aimed at multiple substance abuse problems.

Substance abuse can have an impact from earliest infancy through old age. Some infants are born already compromised through exposure to substances consumed by their mothers during pregnancy. Prenatal exposure to alcohol, tobacco or drugs in utero is linked to psychological, cognitive and physical problems in children. For example, more than 2,000 infants are born every year in the United States with fetal alcohol syndrome, a leading preventable cause of birth defects and developmental disabilities caused by alcohol consumption during pregnancy and other factors.

In addition, more than 6,000 children die each year because of parental smoking, primarily due to sudden infant death syndrome (SIDS) and respiratory infections linked to parental smoking and to low birthweights associated with smoking during pregnancy. Throughout childhood, boys and girls are affected in many other ways by their parents' substance use, from neglect and abuse associated with alcohol and illicit drug abuse to chronic respiratory problems from environmental tobacco smoke.

Adolescence is a period of experimentation with substance use, and teenagers are particularly at risk for involvement in alcohol- and drug-related vehicle injuries. In recent years, there has been a focus on binge drinking, especially among college students. In a survey of more than 14,000 students across 119 college campuses, 51 percent of men and 40 percent of women were classified as binge drinkers—defined in this study as men who drank five or more drinks or women who drank four or more drinks on the same occasion during the previous two-week period. Further, 23 percent of college students were identified as frequent binge drinkers—three or more episodes of binge drinking in the past two weeks.

Because substance use is higher in young adults, men and women in this age group are more likely to experience the problems associated with such use. For example, workplace problems and family disruption can develop during this time. But the long-term health effects of alcohol and cigarette use are most apparent later in life. A lifetime of heavy drinking and/or smoking exacts a heavy toll in chronic health problems and premature death.

Societal Costs of Substance Abuse

The economic cost of substance abuse to the U.S. economy each year is staggering, and it is estimated at over $414 billion. Although specific cost estimates vary across studies because of differences in underlying assumptions and definitions, each study shows substantial economic costs. This is an enormous burden that affects all of society—people who abuse alcohol, tobacco and illicit drugs, and those who do not. This cost includes productivity losses caused by premature death and the inability to perform usual activities, as well as costs related to treatment, crime, destruction of property and other losses.

Alcohol abuse is the most costly, with the total bill to the nation estimated at $166.5 billion in 1995. Using the same economic model, the cost of drug abuse was estimated at $109.9 billion. In a different study, the cost of smoking in 1995 was estimated at $138 billion (Indicator 4). Each substance has different effects on users and on society. The major burden of alcohol abuse is related to productivity losses associated with illness and death; for smoking, the most significant losses are associated with health care costs for myriad adverse health effects and productivity losses due to premature deaths; and for drug-related costs, crime plays the major role.

The costs associated with alcohol and illicit drug abuse are disproportionately attributable to people age 15 to 44. This reflects their higher prevalence of substance abuse problems and greater number of related deaths. The core costs for most other health conditions tend to be concentrated in older age groups.

Taking Action

Substantial government and private efforts are being directed toward combating the nation's substance abuse problem. Federal drug policy has emphasized law enforcement and interdiction to reduce the supply of illicit drugs, but recent trends in public opinion show an increasing interest in prevention and treatment as control measures. Among significant new efforts are the Department of Health and Human Services' youth drug prevention initiative, the Office of National Drug Control Policy's Youth Anti-Drug Media Campaign and the Physician Leadership on

Indicator 4

Economic Costs of Substance Abuse Are High, 1995

Alcohol Abuse

$166.5 billion

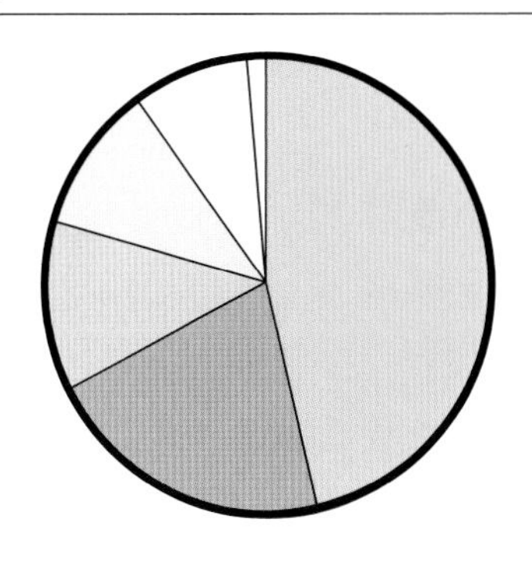

%	Category
46%	Illness
21	Deaths
12	Medical
11	Other Related Costs
9	Crime
1	Special Conditions

Smoking

$138.0 billion

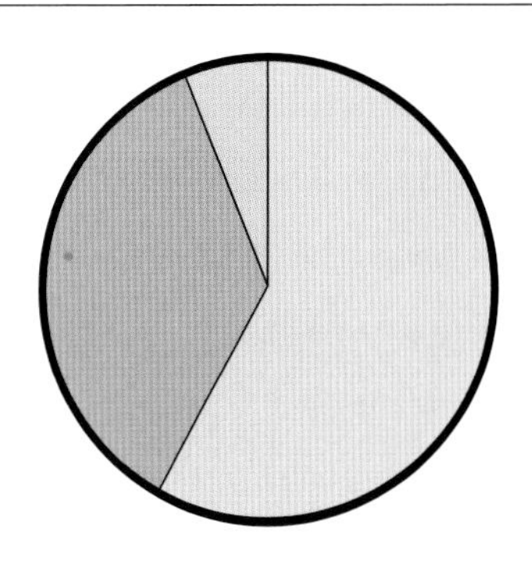

%	Category
58%	Medical
36	Deaths
6	Illness

Drug Abuse

$109.9 billion

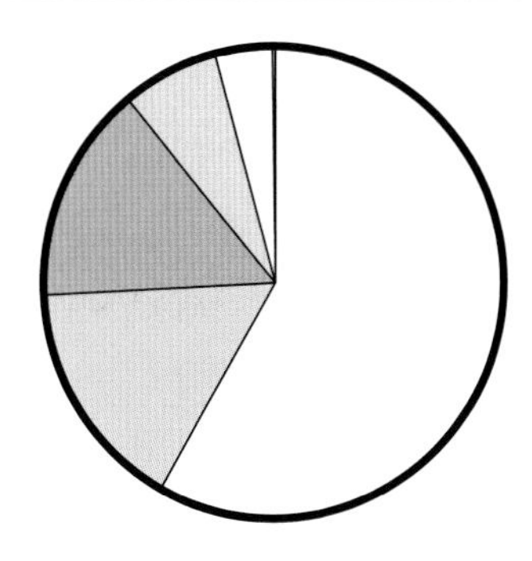

%	Category
58%	Crime
16	Illness
15	Deaths
7	Medical
4	Special Conditions

NOTES: Illness: Value of lost productivity due to illness or injury. Deaths: Value of lost productivity due to premature death. Medical: Health care expenditures, including specialty alcohol and drug abuse services. Other Related Costs: motor vehicle crashes, fire destruction, social welfare administration. Crime: Direct costs of crime (i.e., for the criminal justice system, property damage and private legal defense) and indirect costs (i.e., value of lost productivity related to victims of crime, incarceration and criminal careers). Special Conditions: HIV/AIDS attributable to drug abuse, fetal alcohol syndrome. 1995 estimates of the direct costs of crime for alcohol and drug abuse were calculated by first computing the percentages of 1992 estimated costs of alcohol and drug abuse accounted for by direct costs of crime for alcohol and drug abuse. These percentages were then applied to 1995 estimates of total costs of alcohol and drug abuse.

SOURCES: Alcohol and drug abuse costs: Harwood H, Fountain D, Livermore G. "The Economic Costs of Alcohol and Drug Abuse in the United States, 1992." Rockville, MD: U.S. Department of Health and Human Services, National Institute on Drug Abuse and National Institute on Alcohol Abuse and Alcoholism, 1998. Smoking costs: Unpublished data for 1995 from Rice DP, Institute for Health and Aging, University of California at San Francisco, CA.

National Drug Policy, an all-physician group active in the substance abuse policy arena. Smoking-related efforts have included the unsuccessful attempt by the FDA to regulate the sale of tobacco products to youth and the introduction of comprehensive strategies using funds from state tobacco settlements and excise tax increases. The Leadership to Keep Children Alcohol Free, a national initiative that involves state governors' spouses, is addressing the problem of alcohol use by children age 9 to 15.

There are significant efforts at the state and local levels, including more than 2,000 community coalitions for the prevention of substance abuse, as well as statewide and community coalitions aimed at reducing underage drinking and state tobacco coalitions that work for policy changes. Also at the local level, needle exchange programs to prevent HIV infection are being used to deal with problems associated with illicit drug use.

However, the sheer size of the alcohol and tobacco industries and their influence on the economy—national, state and local—are substantial. In 1998, retail sales of beer, wine and distilled spirits totaled $108 billion, and tobacco sales totaled $59 billion. To help promote these sales, alcohol and tobacco are among the most widely advertised products in the country. In 1997, the alcohol industry spent nearly $1.1 billion on television, radio, print and outdoor advertising, while more than $5.7 billion was spent on tobacco advertising and product promotion.

The alcohol and tobacco industries—with billions of dollars in retail sales and advertising and product promotion—have a powerful influence on public opinion and government policies regarding substance abuse. Some of these policies regulate, tax and otherwise limit the distribution of alcohol and tobacco products, while others create tax write-offs for advertising them. In addition, alcohol and tobacco advertising targets some of the very groups the public health community is trying to reach with its health promotion activities.

Monitoring Change

The U.S. Public Health Service has established objectives for decreasing the use of alcohol, tobacco and illicit drugs as part of a major effort to increase the healthy life span of Americans, reduce health disparities among population groups and achieve access to preventive services for all. The federal government's *Healthy People 2000: National Health Promotion and Disease Prevention Objectives* and the *Healthy People 2010 Objectives* are blueprints for action that include specific measurable targets for different age groups. Two charts of *Healthy People 2000* objectives related to substance abuse are presented at the end of this report to provide a snapshot of the current status of progress toward these objectives. National data and information on important population subgroups, such as youth, are emphasized.

A number of recent developments may affect substance use, abuse and dependency, as well as prevention, treatment and progress toward the national objectives. For example, factors that may lead to decreases in the overall rates for some substances include the aging of the population; the growing efforts to curb youth access to alcohol and tobacco products; and raising excise taxes and new state and federal funding for youth-oriented substance abuse counteradvertising. The elimination of substance abuse as a basis for eligibility for Social Security Insurance (SSI), Social Security Disability Insurance (SSDI) benefits and subsequent Medicaid and Medicare coverage, optional drug testing and work requirements under the 1996 Welfare Reform Act are likely to increase the demand for treatment services. In addition, the rapid expansion of managed care programs for substance abuse will affect the service delivery of prevention and treatment programs. Finally, increased understanding of the neurobiological bases of addiction has the potential to yield more effective treatment and prevention programs. However, it may take some time before the effects and implications of these developments become apparent.

Overview

The Context of Substance Abuse

A HEALTH AND SOCIAL PROBLEM

Institute of Medicine. *Dispelling the Myths about Addiction: Strategies to Increase Understanding and Strengthen Research.* Washington, DC: National Academy Press, 1997.

Institute of Medicine. *Pathways of Addiction: Opportunities in Drug Abuse Research.* Washington, DC: National Academy Press, 1996.

National Institute on Alcohol Abuse and Alcoholism. *Tenth Special Report to the U.S. Congress on Alcohol and Health from the Secretary of Health and Human Services.* Rockville, MD, 2000.

USE, ABUSE AND DEPENDENCE

Grant BF. "Prevalence and Correlates of Alcohol Use and DSM-IV Alcohol Dependence in the United States: Results of the National Longitudinal Alcohol Epidemiologic Survey." *Journal of Studies on Alcohol,* 58(5): 464–473, 1997.

Kandel D, Chen K, Warner LA, Kessler RC and Grant B. "Prevalence and Demographic Correlates of Symptoms of Last Year Dependence on Alcohol, Nicotine, Marijuana and Cocaine in the U.S. Population." *Drug and Alcohol Dependence,* 44(1): 11–29, 1997.

Lowinson JH (ed.). *Substance Abuse: A Comprehensive Textbook.* Baltimore, MD: Williams and Wilkins, 1997.

Bierut L, Dinwiddie S, Begleiter H et al. "Familial Transmission of Substance Dependence: Alcohol, Marijuana, Cocaine and Habitual Smoking: A Report from the Collaborative Study on the Genetics of Alcoholism." *Archives of General Psychiatry,* 55(11): 982–988, 1998.

HISTORICAL TRENDS IN CONSUMPTION AND POLICY

Houston T and Kaufman NJ. "Tobacco Control in the 21st Century: Searching for Answers in a Sea of Change." *Journal of the American Medical Association,* 284(6):752–753, 2000.

Musto DF. "Alcohol in American History." *Scientific American,* April 1996: 78–83.

Musto DF. "Perception and Regulation of Drug Use: The Rise and Fall of the Tide." *Annals of Internal Medicine,* 123(6): 468–469, 1995.

ALL SEGMENTS OF SOCIETY AFFECTED

U.S. Substance Abuse and Mental Health Services Administration, Office of Applied Studies. *Prevalence of Substance Use among Racial and Ethnic Subgroups in the United States 1991–1993.* Rockville, MD, 1998.

U.S. Substance Abuse and Mental Health Services Administration, Office of Applied Studies. *Substance Abuse among Women in the United States.* Rockville, MD, 1997.

SOCIETAL COSTS OF SUBSTANCE ABUSE

Harwood H, Fountain D and Livermore G. "The Economic Costs of Alcohol and Drug Abuse in the United States 1992." Rockville MD: U.S. Department of Health and Human Services, National Institute on Drug Abuse and National Institute on Alcohol Abuse and Alcoholism, 1998.

TAKING ACTION

Join Together. A National Resource for Communities Fighting Substance Abuse. *Promising Strategies: Results of the Fourth National Survey on Community Efforts to Reduce Substance Abuse and Gun Violence.* Boston, MA, 1999.

National Institute on Drug Abuse. *Preventing Drug Use among Children and Adolescents: A Research-Based Guide,* 1997.

MONITORING CHANGE

National Center for Health Statistics. *Healthy People 2000 Review, 1997.* Hyattsville, MD: Public Health Service, 1997.

Lewin-VHI, Inc. "Labor Market Conditions, Socioeconomic Factors and the Growth of Applications and Awards for SSDI and SSI Disability Benefits" (Final Report). Washington, DC: The Office of the Assistant Secretary for Planning and Evaluation and the Social Security Administration, 1995.

Patterns of Use

- Most Americans are aware of the risks associated with substance abuse, but the perception of risk rises with age. Each successive age group from age 12 to 17 to 35 and older reports increasingly greater risk associated with substance use.
- By the 8th grade, 52 percent of adolescents have consumed alcohol, 41 percent have smoked cigarettes and 20 percent have used marijuana.
- Frequent or heavy use of alcohol, tobacco and cocaine remained fairly stable in the 1990s; frequent marijuana use increased.
- Males are almost four times as likely as females to be heavy drinkers, nearly one and a half times as likely to smoke a pack or more of cigarettes a day and twice as likely to smoke marijuana weekly. These gender differences are closing among youth.
- Substance abuse is a chronic, relapsing health condition. Substance abusers may be in treatment multiple times—or make repeated attempts to quit on their own—before they are successful.

Perception of Risk

Most Americans recognize the substantial health risks associated with the use of alcohol, tobacco and illicit drugs. Even so, tobacco and illicit drug use increased among 8th, 10th and 12th graders between the early 1990s and 1996, although these trends in use started to shift downward in 1997. Notable exceptions are the sharp increases in ecstasy use at all grade levels and the increase in heroin use by 12th graders and steriod use by 10th graders. Alcohol use has been more stable during the 1990s, but there were slight declines—in annual and monthly alcohol use for 8th and 10th graders in 1998—as well as an increase in binge drinking for 8th graders between 1998 and 1999.

Drug use among those age 18 and older has been fairly stable, with the exception of an increase between 1994 and 1996 in those age 18 to 25 who reported using an illicit drug in the past month, as well as an increase in the number of new heroin users in this age group.

The increases in substance use among youth between the early 1990s and 1996 were linked to decreases in the perception of potential harm from use of many substances, particularly marijuana (Indicator 5). However, for many substances these decreases in the perception of potential harm have leveled off or reversed. As expected, as perception of risk has increased, use rates have begun to shift downward.

In addition, other factors are believed to have contributed to the increases in substance use among youth in the early 1990s. Researchers use the term "generational forgetting" to describe the notion that many young people have not seen the dangerous consequences of drug use among the cohort that preceded them because that group had relatively low levels of drug use. Additional factors were the decline in the prevalence of warnings and anti-drug messages from the media, parents and schools; the appearance of pro-use messages from the entertainment world, especially the music industry; and tobacco and alcohol product advertising and promotion. Finally, the increase in cigarette smoking among youth in the early 1990s may have contributed to the increased use of drugs, particularly marijuana. A turnaround in these factors may also be attributable to recent decreases in substance use among youth.

Not all substances are perceived as being equally risky. Overall, more individuals report a greater risk of harm associated with regular use of cocaine or heroin than with

Indicator 5

Youth Perception of Risk Varies by Substance

Percent of High School Seniors Who Believe Substance Use Is Very Risky

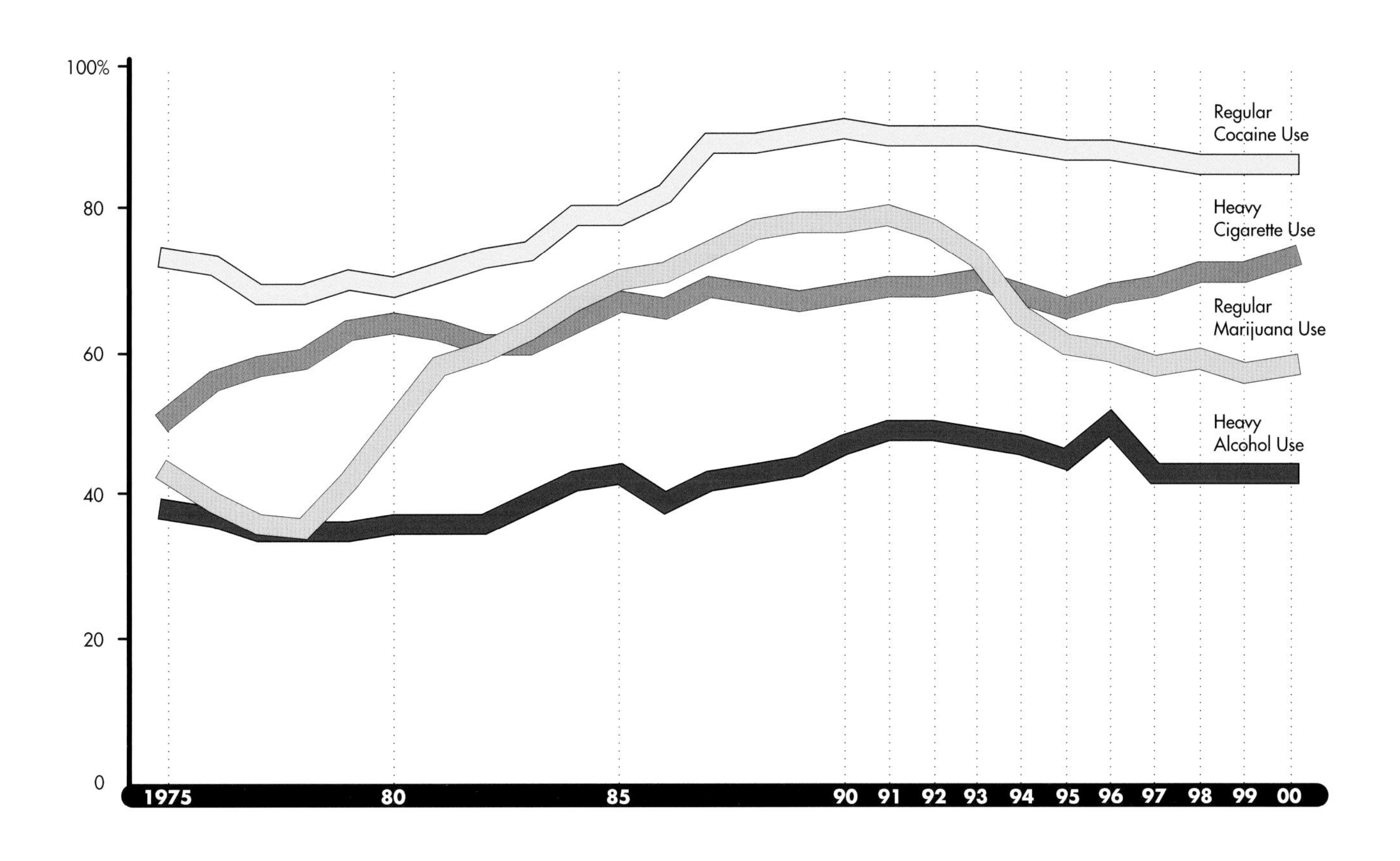

In Percent

	1975	80	85	90	91	92	93	94	95	96	97	98	99	00
Regular Cocaine Use	73	69	79	91	90	90	90	89	88	88	87	86	86	86
Heavy Cigarette Use	51	64	67	68	69	69	70	68	66	68	69	71	71	73
Regular Marijuana Use	43	50	70	78	79	77	73	65	61	60	58	59	57	58
Heavy Alcohol Use	38	36	43	47	49	49	48	47	45	50	43	43	43	43

NOTE: Data are percentages of high school seniors who see "great risk" of harm from smoking one or more packs of cigarettes each day, having five or more drinks once or twice each weekend, smoking marijuana regularly or using cocaine regularly.

SOURCE: National survey results from the *Monitoring the Future Study*, 2000, as reported in: The University of Michigan News and Information Services. "Ecstasy Use Rises Sharply among Teens in 2000; Use of Many Other Drugs Stays Steady, but Significant Declines Are Reported for Some," December 13, 2000. Table 9.

Perception of Risk (continued)

regular use of marijuana, which is viewed as less risky. In addition, regular or heavier use of alcohol or illicit drugs is seen as riskier than occasional or experimental use. Also, there are differences in perception of risk by age, and several substances are perceived as increasingly risky by each successive age group. For example, the number of individuals reporting perceptions of great risk associated with having four or five drinks every day, smoking one or more packs of cigarettes a day or using cocaine on a monthly or weekly basis increases with each successive age cohort.

While the majority of young people disapprove of smoking a pack or more a day, the disapproval rate declined between the early 1990s and 1996 for 8th and 10th graders; in 1997, it was at its lowest level among 12th graders in nearly two decades (Indicator 6). At the same time, there was a significant increase in cigarette smoking among high school students. This increase in smoking rates appears to have leveled off in 1997 for 8th and 10th graders and has declined substantially for all three grade levels since then.

Perception of risk is important because more than 80 percent of adult smokers began smoking before age 18. Young people who smoke are 16 times more likely to drink heavily and 10 times more likely to use illicit drugs than their nonsmoking peers.

A growing number of American adults are also concerned about environmental tobacco smoke—the exposure of nonsmokers to cigarette smoke in people's homes, at work and in public places. According to a 1997 nationwide Gallup poll, 55 percent of the public believes that secondhand smoke is very harmful; in 1994, only 36 percent thought it was very harmful.

Indicator 6

Disapproval of Heavy Smoking Reverses Its Downward Trend among Youth

Percent of 8th, 10th and 12th Graders Who Disapprove of Heavy Smoking

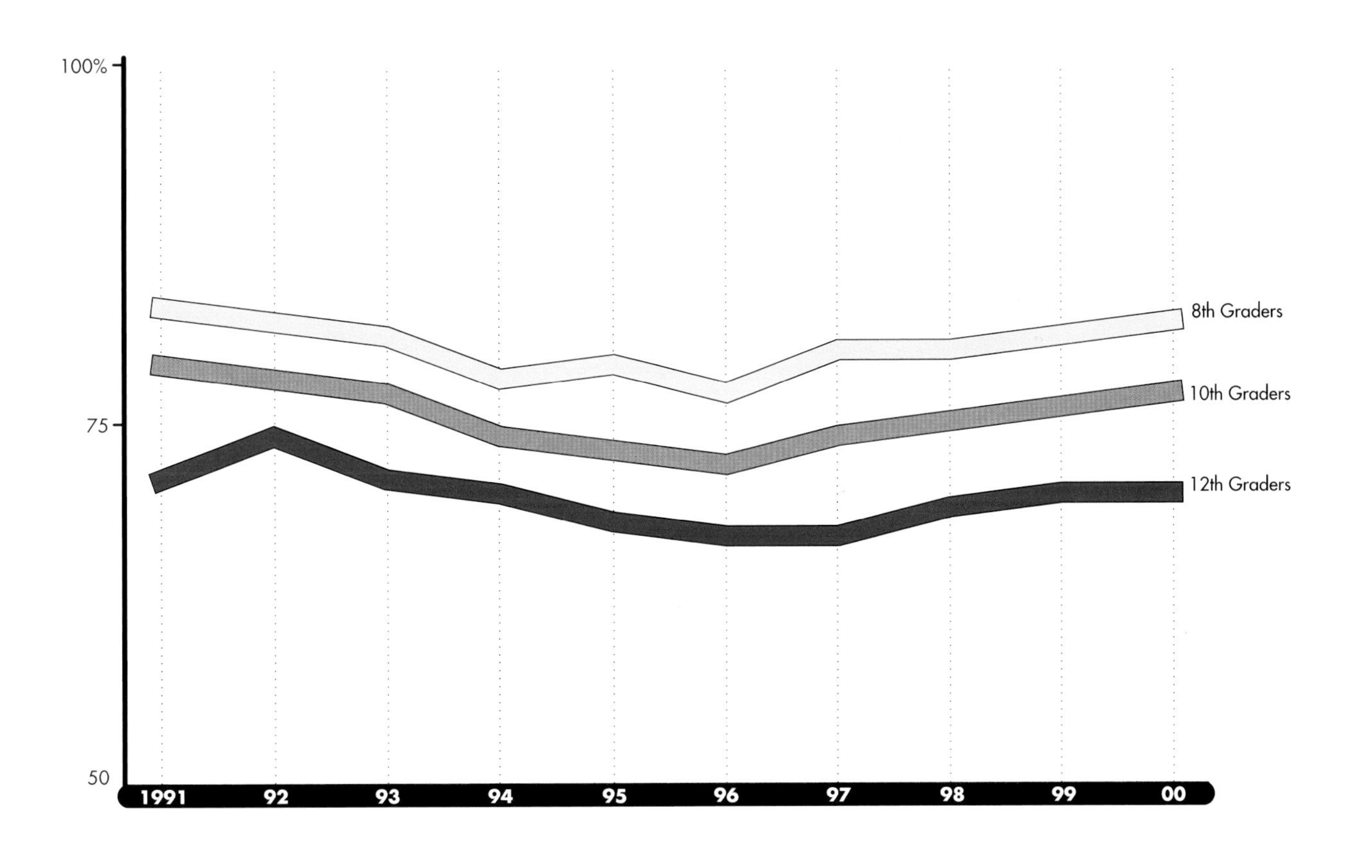

In Percent

	1991	92	93	94	95	96	97	98	99	00
8th Graders	83	82	81	78	79	77	80	80	81	82
10th Graders	79	78	77	74	73	72	74	75	76	77
12th Graders	71	74	71	70	68	67	67	69	70	70

NOTE: Heavy smoking is smoking one or more packs of cigarettes per day.

SOURCE: National survey results from the *Monitoring the Future Study*, 2000, as reported in: The University of Michigan News and Information Services. "Ecstasy Use Rises Sharply among Teens in 2000; Use of Many Other Drugs Stays Steady, but Significant Declines Are Reported for Some," December 13, 2000. Table 11.

Implications of Early Use

Age is one of the most important factors explaining the likelihood of using alcohol, tobacco and illicit drugs. It also is related to subsequent patterns of use and problems associated with use. New research suggests that significant changes in drug awareness take place between ages 12 and 13. Thirteen-year-olds are three times as likely to know how to obtain marijuana or to know someone who uses illicit drugs than are 12-year-olds. Young adults—age 18 to 25—are the group most likely to engage in heavy alcohol use, smoke cigarettes and use illicit drugs (Indicator 7).

Many young people begin to experiment with alcohol, tobacco and illicit drugs at very early ages, although not all who try drugs once or twice continue to use them. By the 8th grade, 52 percent of youth have tried alcohol, 41 percent have smoked cigarettes and 20 percent have tried marijuana (Indicator 8). By the 12th grade, about 80 percent have used alcohol, 63 percent have smoked cigarettes and 49 percent have used marijuana. Most people begin smoking as adolescents, and among youths who smoke, the average age of initiation is 12½. Cigar smoking also starts at a young age. More than one-quarter of students in grades 9–12—and more than one-half of teenage cigarette smokers—had smoked at least one cigar in the past year.

Numbers of New Initiates Increasing, 1990–1997

Number of Persons Who First Used Each Substance during Each Year in Thousands

	1990	1997
Alcohol	3,342	4,199
Cigarettes	2,575	3,108
Daily Cigarette	1,473	2,134
Marijuana	1,423	2,114
Cocaine	605	730
Inhalant	364	708
Hallucinogen	620	1,094
Heroin	66	81

SOURCE: U.S. Substance Abuse and Mental Health Services Administration, Office of Applied Studies. *Summary of Findings from the 1998 National Household Survey on Drug Abuse.* Rockville, MD, 1999. Tables 41–48, pp. 105–112.

Young people are starting to use illicit substances earlier. The rising prevalence of marijuana use during the first half of the 1990s was driven by the increasing rate of new use among youths age 12 to 17. Declines in the mean age of first use of cocaine and heroin were accompanied by an upward trend in the rate of new cocaine and heroin users among the 12- to 17-year-old

Indicator 7

Young Adults Use Substances More than Any Other Group, 1998

Percent of Users in Past Month

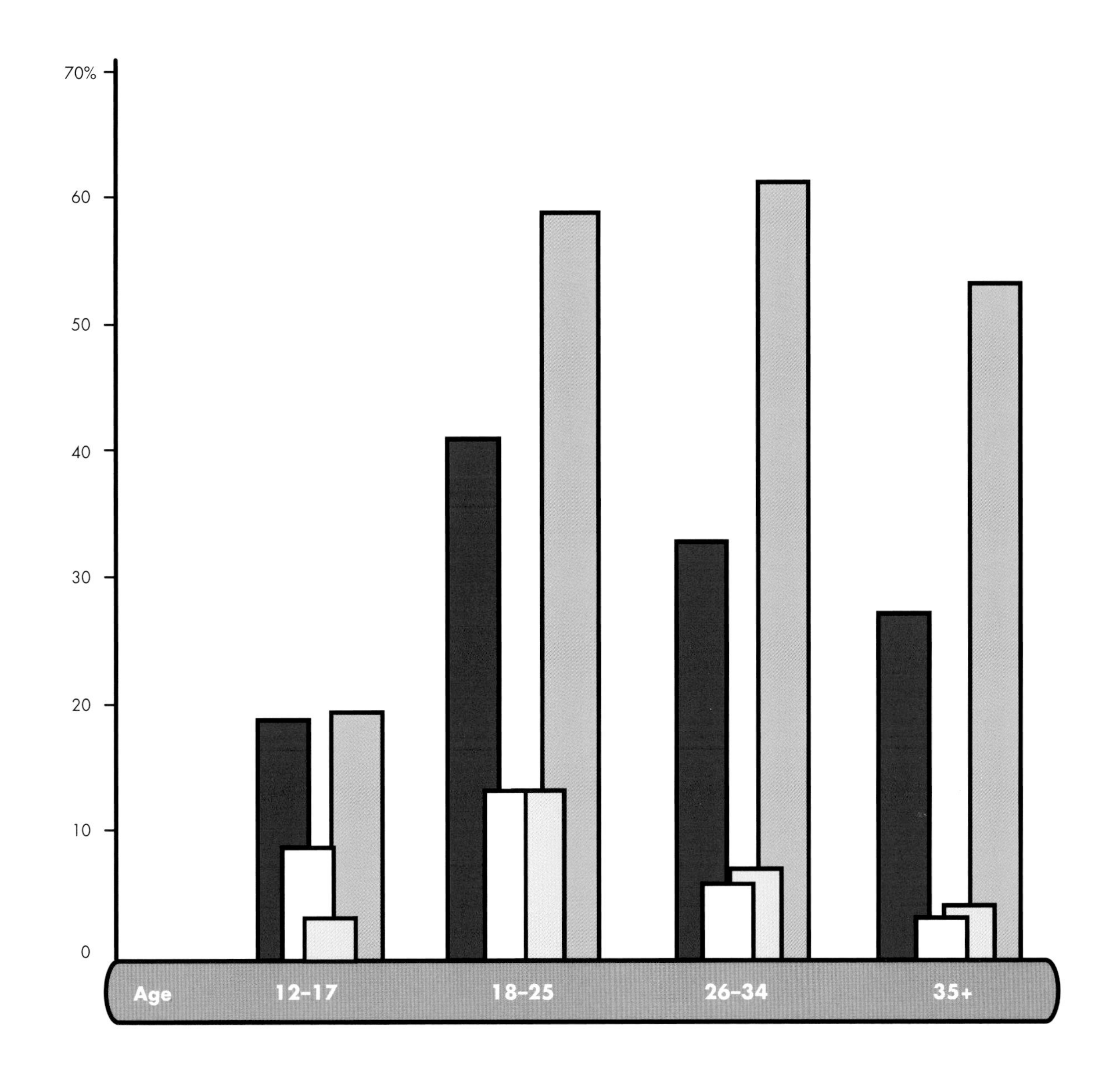

In Percent

	12-17	18-25	26-34	35+
Cigarettes	19	41	33	27
Marijuana	9	13	6	3
Heavy Alcohol	3	13	7	4
Alcohol	20	59	61	53

NOTE: Heavy alcohol use is having five or more drinks on the same occasion on each of five or more days in the past 30 days.

SOURCE: U.S. Substance Abuse and Mental Health Services Administration, Office of Applied Studies. *Summary of Findings from the 1998 National Household Survey on Drug Abuse*, Rockville, MD, 1999. Tables 32–37, pp. 95–100.

Implications of Early Use (continued)

age group between 1990 and 1997. Young people age 12 to 17 and 18 to 25 account for the majority of the increase in the numbers of new initiates for many substances in the 1990s (see table).

Because alcohol, tobacco and marijuana are often tried before other illicit drugs such as cocaine, heroin or hallucinogens, they often are referred to as "gateway drugs." Tobacco use among adolescents is a particularly powerful predictor of other drug use, especially among females. Alcohol is a strong predictor of progression into other drug use for males. Fortunately, however, many youth who use cigarettes, alcohol or marijuana never try other illicit drugs.

The age when young people first start using alcohol, tobacco and illicit drugs is a powerful predictor of later alcohol and drug problems, especially if use begins before age 15. People who begin smoking or using alcohol when they are very young are more likely to be heavy users of these substances later on. In fact, more than 40 percent of those who started drinking at age 14 or younger developed alcohol dependence, compared with 10 percent of those who began drinking at age 20 or older.

High school students who use illicit drugs are more likely to experience difficulties in school, in their personal relationships and in their mental and physical health. By age 20, a time when young people may be in school, entering the work force and beginning to get married and have families, these and other problems related to alcohol and drug dependence typically become apparent.

Indicator 8

Substance Use Declines among 8th Graders, 2000

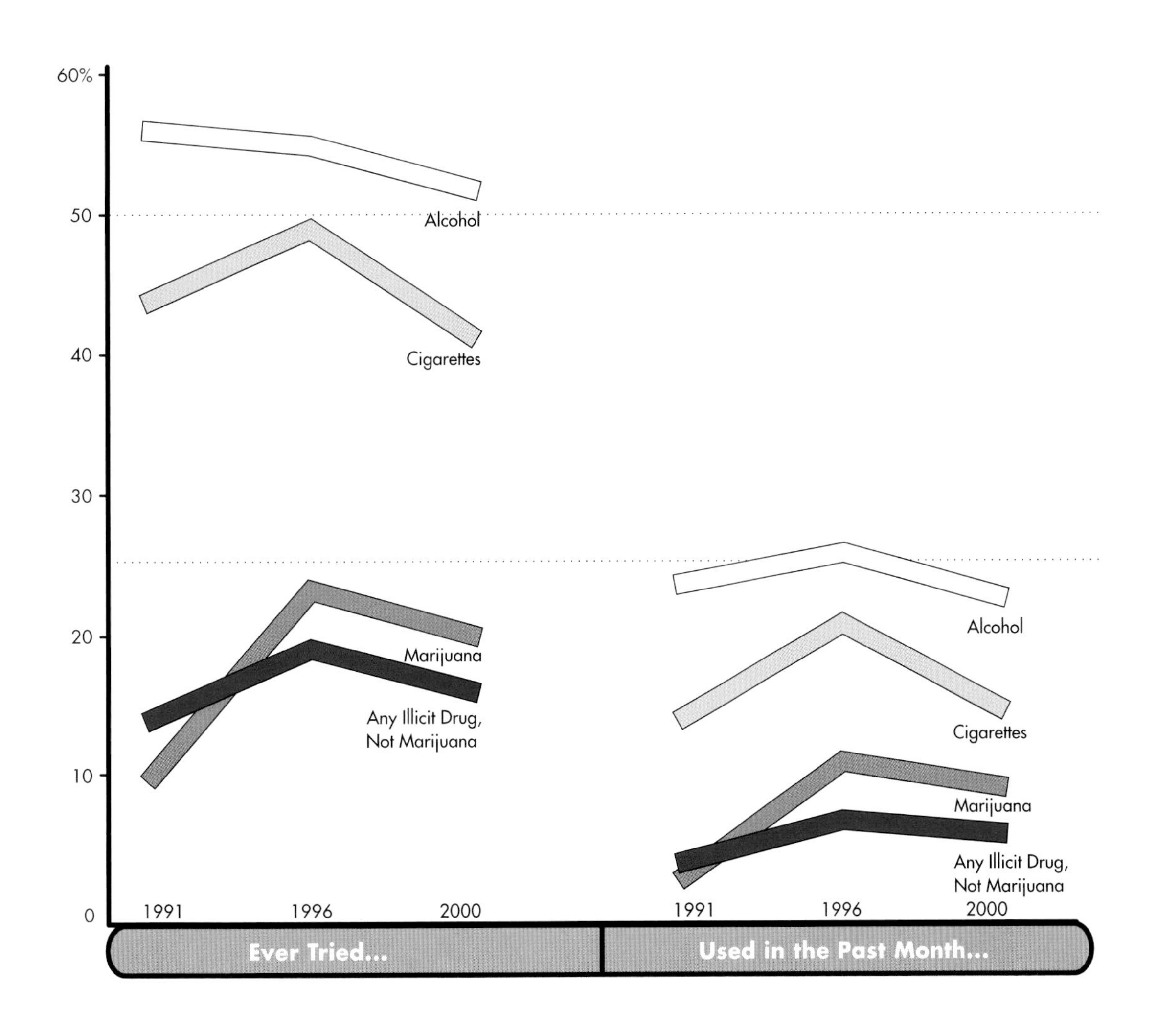

%	Ever	Past Month	Ever	Past Month	Ever	Past Month
Alcohol	56	24	55	26	52	22
Cigarettes	44	14	49	21	41	15
Marijuana	10	3	23	11	20	9
Any Illicit Drug, Not Marijuana	14	4	19	7	16	6
	1991		**1996**		**2000**	

NOTE: Data for alcohol use are from 1993, 1996 and 2000 because 1991 data are not comparable to 1996 or 2000 data due to a change in the wording of the question.

SOURCE: National survey results from the *Monitoring the Future Study*, 2000, as reported in: The University of Michigan News and Information Services. "Ecstasy Use Rises Sharply among Teens in 2000; Use of Many Other Drugs Stays Steady, but Significant Declines Are Reported for Some," December 13, 2000. Tables 1 and 2.

Trends in Use

The number of frequent, heavy users of alcohol, cigarettes and illicit drugs is sizable. The definition of heavy use varies, depending on the substance. Binge drinking involves consuming five or more drinks per occasion in the past month, and heavy drinking usually means consuming five or more drinks per occasion on five or more days in the past month; heavy smoking is often defined as smoking a pack or more of cigarettes a day during the past month; and heavy drug use may be considered to be at least weekly use in the past month.

Trends in Alcohol Use, U.S. Household Population
Percent Reporting Past Month Use

	1985	1990	1994	1998
Any Alcohol Use	60%	53%	54%	52%
Binge Alcohol Use	20	14	17	16
Heavy Alcohol Use	8	6	6	6

NOTES: Binge alcohol use is having five or more drinks on the same occasion at least once in the past 30 days. Heavy alcohol use is having five or more drinks on the same occasion on each of five or more days in the past 30 days. Data are reported for those age 12 and older and include individuals who do not drink.

SOURCE: U.S. Substance Abuse and Mental Health Services Administration, Office of Applied Studies. *Summary of Findings from the 1998 National Household Survey on Drug Abuse.* Rockville, MD, 1999. Table 30, p. 93.

To illustrate how much heavy drinkers actually consume, half of the alcohol consumed in this country is accounted for by the 10 percent of the population that drinks the most heavily. The percentage of the population age 12 and older that drinks any alcohol or engages in binge alcohol use and heavy alcohol use has declined significantly since 1985 (see table). Of the 113 million current users of alcohol in 1998, 33 million (29 percent) were binge drinkers, and 11 million (10 percent) were heavy drinkers. The statistics are even more alarming for those age 12 to 20: Of the 10.4 million current drinkers, 5.1 million (49 percent) were binge drinkers and 2.3 million (22 percent) were heavy drinkers.

Use and level of use of alcohol are strongly associated with tobacco and illicit drug use (Indicator 9). Among heavy drinkers, two-thirds also smoked cigarettes, more than one-quarter used marijuana and one-seventh used other illicit drugs. Nondrinkers were the least likely to smoke cigarettes or use any illicit drug, including marijuana. Similarly, among youths age 12 to 17, 30 percent of those who had at least one drink in the past month (not heavy or binge drinking) had used an illicit drug, compared with 3 percent of those who did not drink; among those who used cigarettes in the past month, 39 percent had also used an illicit drug, compared with only 3 percent of their nonsmoking peers.

Indicator 9

Heavy and Binge Drinking Linked to Cigarette and Illicit Drug Use, 1998

Percent Using in Past Month

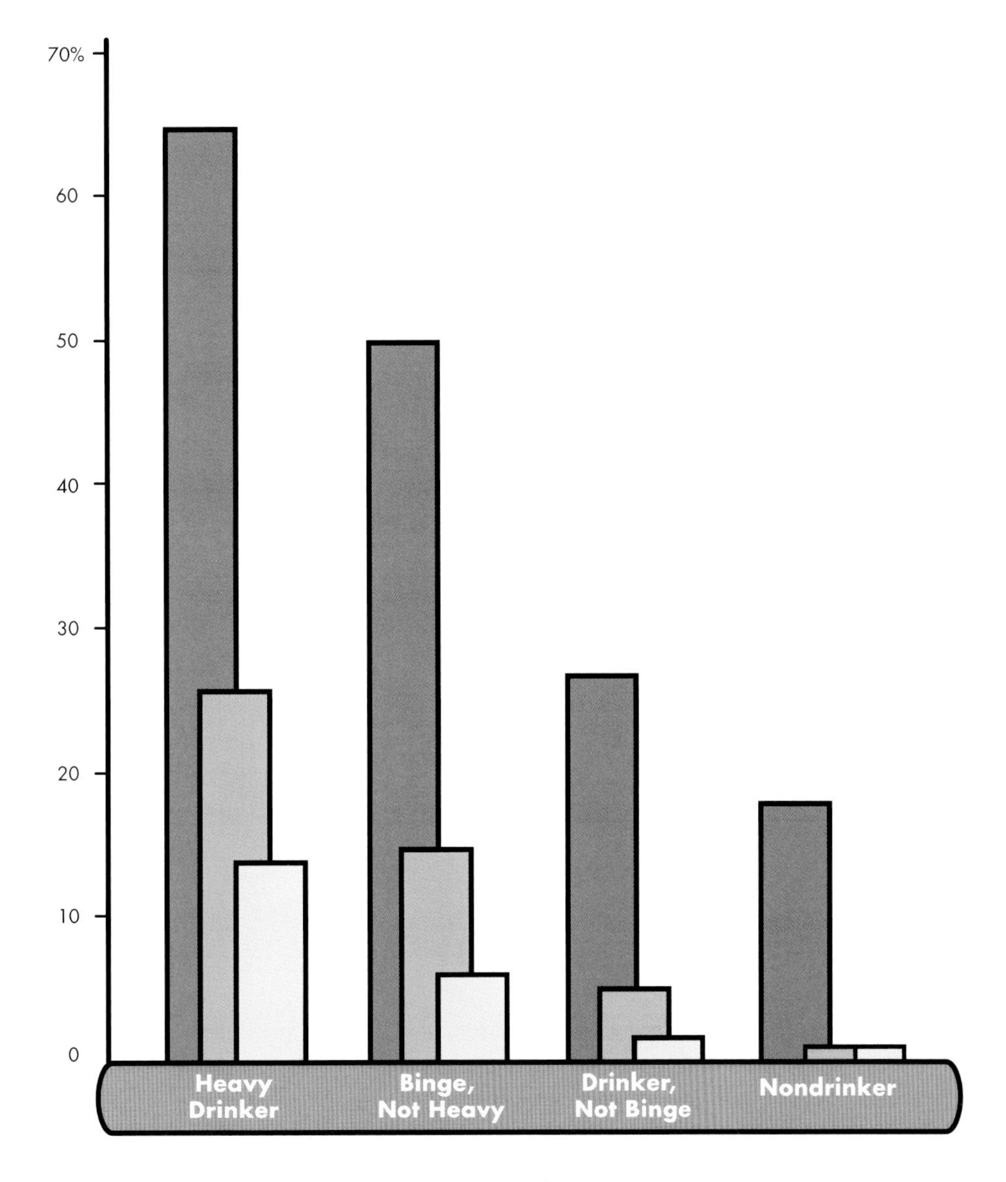

In Percent

	Heavy Drinker	Binge, Not Heavy	Drinker, Not Binge	Nondrinker
Cigarettes	65	50	27	18
Marijuana	26	15	5	1
Any Illicit Drug, Not Marijuana	14	6	2	1

NOTES: Heavy alcohol use is having five or more drinks on the same occasion on each of five or more days in the past 30 days; binge drinking is having five or more drinks on the same occasion on at least one day in the past 30 days. Cigarette use refers to past month use. Any illicit drug use other than marijuana indicates use at least once in the past month of cocaine (including crack), inhalants, hallucinogens (including PCP and LSD), heroin or any prescription-type psychotherapeutic used nonmedically, regardless of marijuana use. Data are reported for those age 12 and older.

SOURCE: U.S. Substance Abuse and Mental Health Services Administration, Office of Applied Studies. *Summary of Findings from the 1998 National Household Survey on Drug Abuse*. Rockville, MD, 1999. Table 38, p. 101.

The decrease in the number of people using illicit drugs since the late 1970s has been dramatic. At that time, almost 40 percent of high school seniors were using illicit drugs. In contrast, in 2000, 25 percent of high school seniors reported using drugs in the past 30 days. For people age 18 to 25—the age group with the highest rates of illicit drug use—past month marijuana use peaked at 36 percent in 1979 and fell to 14 percent in 1998. Past month cocaine use among this age group also peaked in 1979 at 10 percent and dropped to 2 percent in 1998. Overall, the proportion of the population reporting past month use of any illicit drugs dropped from 14 percent in 1979 to 6 percent in 1998.

However, there were overall increases in past month use of heroin and hallucinogens between 1993 and 1997, although this trend appears to have halted in 1998. The number of people who reported weekly or monthly marijuana use also increased in the 1990s. The number of cocaine users reporting weekly or monthly use was relatively stable during this time (Indicator 10). Heavy drug use remains a particularly difficult problem in many urban areas, where hard-core users and drug-related crime are concentrated.

Cigarette use has decreased overall since the 1960s. The proportion of the adult population that smoked in the past month decreased from 42 percent in 1965 to 25 percent in 1997. Despite this overall decline in smokers, the proportion of heavy smokers has not changed much. Among youth, rates of daily smoking and rates of smoking at least half a pack of cigarettes per day reached a peak for 8th and 10th graders in 1996 and for 12th graders in 1997. By 2000, there were substantial declines in each of these measures at each grade level. Smokeless tobacco use has remained relatively stable in recent years; in 1998, about 3 percent of the population reported past month use of such tobacco. Current cigar use, however, is on the increase, rising from 5.9 percent of the population in 1997 to 6.9 percent in 1998.

Indicator 10

Heavier Marijuana Use Increases, Heavier Cocaine Use Is Stable in the '90s

Number of Users Ages 12 and Older in Millions

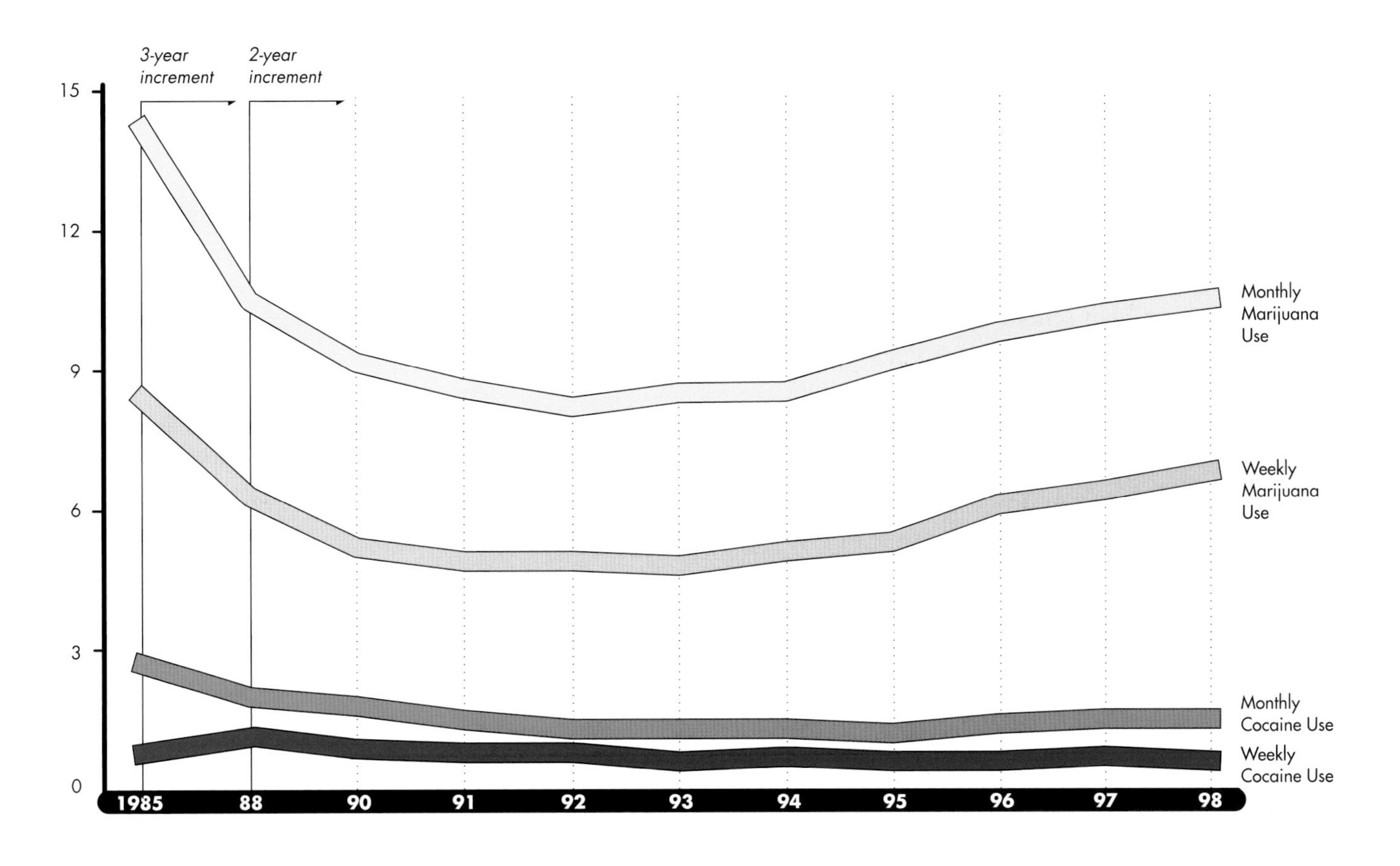

In Millions

	1985	88	90	91	92	93	94	95	96	97	98
Monthly Marijuana Use	14.2	10.5	9.1	8.6	8.2	8.5	8.5	9.2	9.8	10.2	10.5
Weekly Marijuana Use	8.4	6.3	5.2	4.9	4.9	4.8	5.1	5.3	6.1	6.4	6.8
Monthly Cocaine Use	2.7	2.0	1.8	1.5	1.3	1.3	1.3	1.2	1.4	1.5	1.5
Weekly Cocaine Use	.8	1.1	.9	.8	.8	.6	.7	.6	.6	.7	.6

NOTES: Monthly use is equivalent to use on 12 or more days in the past year. Weekly use is equivalent to use on 51 or more days in the past year.

SOURCES: For 1988 and 1990: U.S. Substance Abuse and Mental Health Services Administration, Office of Applied Studies. *Preliminary Results from the 1996 National Household Survey on Drug Abuse*, Rockville, MD, 1997.

For 1985 and 1991–1998: U.S. Substance Abuse and Mental Health Services Administration, Office of Applied Studies. *Summary of Findings from the 1998 National Household Survey on Drug Abuse*, Rockville, MD, 1999. Table 18A, p. 80.

Demographic Differences in Heavy Use

Population groups differ in their rates of heavy use of alcohol, tobacco and illicit drugs. These variations are most apparent when considered by race/ethnicity, gender, education and geographic region.

Among high school seniors, whites are most likely and blacks least likely to be heavy drinkers and smokers; Hispanics fall in between (Indicators 11 and 12). After years of significant declines, cigarette smoking by black and Hispanic adolescents increased in the 1990s. The increase in smoking was particularly dramatic for African American youths, who experienced an 80 percent increase in smoking between 1991 and 1997. Since then, declines in smoking have been reported for white, black and Hispanic youth.

While American Indians and Alaskan Natives have the highest rates of tobacco use, they are less likely than whites to be heavy smokers. Among smokers, whites smoke more cigarettes per day than any other racial/ethnic minority group. Further, white smokers are more likely to smoke on a daily basis than African American, Asian American and Hispanic smokers.

The percentage of heavy drinkers varies across racial groups. Data from 1998 show that Hispanics are most likely to engage in heavy alcohol use, followed by whites and blacks (see table). Blacks are more likely to report using drugs on a weekly basis than whites, Hispanics or other racial/ethnic groups.

Heavy Alcohol Use Varies across Racial Groups
Percent Reporting Past Month Heavy Alcohol Use

Race/Ethnicity	1991	1993	1998
White	7%	8%	6%
Black	4	3	5
Hispanic	7	6	7
Other	3	2	5

NOTES: Heavy alcohol use is having five or more drinks on the same occasion on each of five or more days in the past 30 days. Data are reported for those age 12 and older.

SOURCE: U.S. Substance Abuse and Mental Health Administration, Office of Applied Studies. *Summary of Findings from the 1998 National Household Survey on Drug Abuse.* Rockville, MD, 1999. Table 16, p. 78.

There also are differences in substance use by gender. Among high school seniors, college students and young adults, males are much more likely than females to be heavy drinkers. After nearly two decades of higher smoking rates among female high school seniors, males have had higher rates of current smoking than females since 1991. In 1998, males in the 8th, 10th and 12th grades had higher rates of

Indicator 11

Heavy Alcohol Use by Youth Varies by Race and Ethnic Group

Percent of High School Seniors Who Are Heavy Users

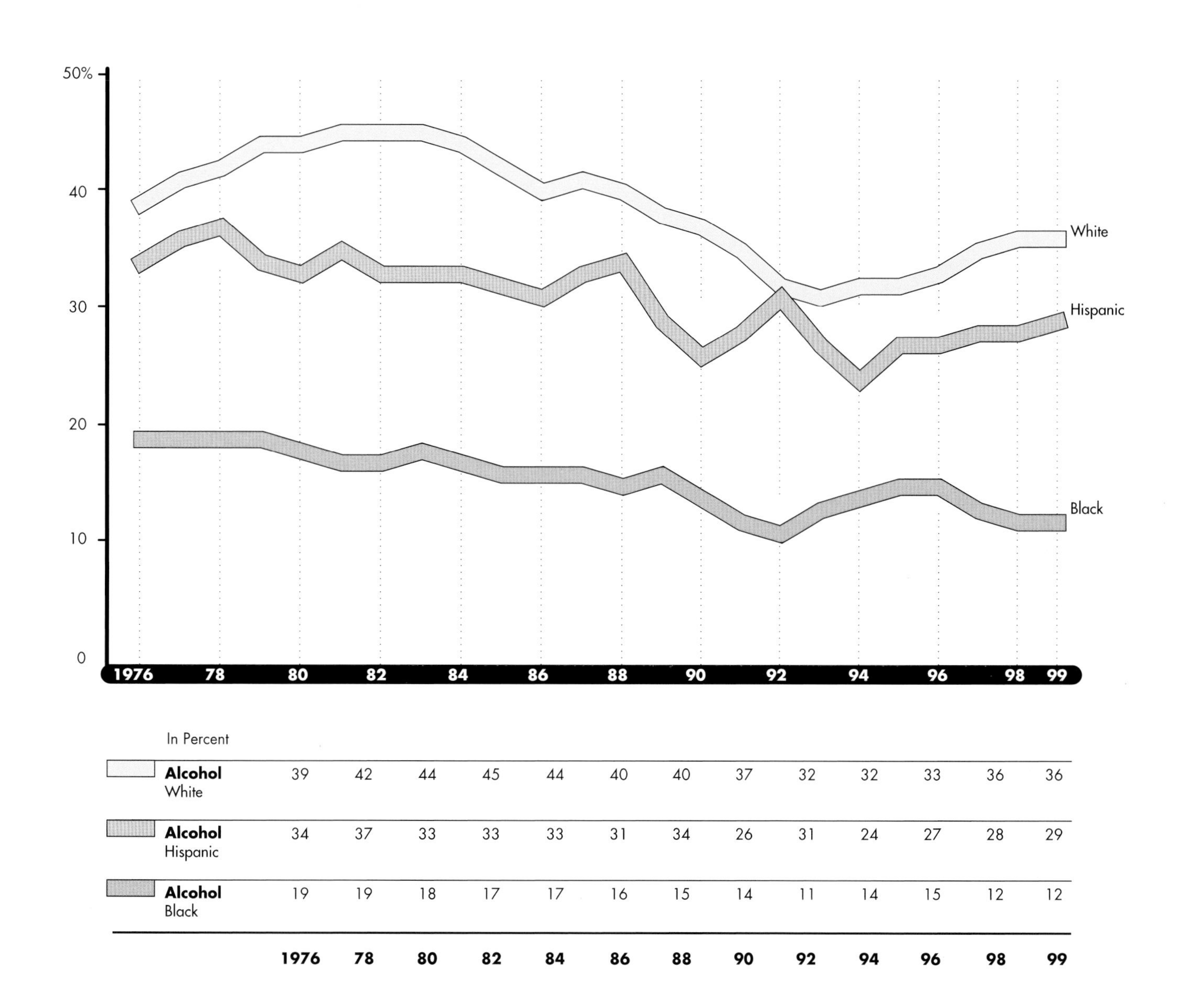

In Percent	1976	78	80	82	84	86	88	90	92	94	96	98	99
Alcohol White	39	42	44	45	44	40	40	37	32	32	33	36	36
Alcohol Hispanic	34	37	33	33	33	31	34	26	31	24	27	28	29
Alcohol Black	19	19	18	17	17	16	15	14	11	14	15	12	12

NOTES: Each point plotted is the mean of the specified year and the previous year. Hispanic data are derived from self-reports. Heavy alcohol use is five or more drinks in a row on one or more occasions in the past two weeks.

SOURCE: Johnston LD, O'Malley PM, Bachman JG. *National Survey Results on Drug Use from the Monitoring the Future Study, 1975–1999. Volume I: Secondary School Students.* Rockville, MD: National Institute on Drug Abuse, 2000. Table D–45, p. 460.

Demographic Differences in Heavy Use (continued)

heavier smoking—half a pack or more daily—than females. While there are fewer differences by gender for 8th and 10th graders, male high school seniors, college students and young adults are more likely than their female counterparts to use most illicit drugs and to be frequent or heavy users.

Across people of all ages, males are four times as likely as females to be heavy drinkers and 1.3 times as likely to smoke a pack or more of cigarettes a day. Males also are twice as likely to engage in frequent marijuana use, but there is no significant gender difference in frequent cocaine use (see table).

Heavy and Frequent Use Higher among Males, 1998
Percent Reporting Use

	Male	Female
Past Month Heavy Alcohol Use	10%	2%
Past Month Heavy Cigarette Use	13	10
Past Year Frequent Marijuana Use	4	2
Past Year Frequent Cocaine Use	0.3	0.2

NOTES: Heavy alcohol use is having five or more drinks on the same occasion on each of 5 or more days in the past 30 days; heavy cigarette use is a pack or more a day; and frequent marijuana and cocaine use is use on 51 or more days in the past year.

SOURCES: U.S. Substance Abuse and Mental Health Services Administration, Office of Applied Studies. *Summary of Findings from the 1998 National Household Survey on Drug Abuse*. Rockville, MD, 1999. Table 16, p. 87; 1998 Main Findings, Table 8.6, p. 120; 1998 Population Estimates, Tables 20A and 21A, pp. 109 and 115.

Where people live and their level of education also relate to heavy substance use. Heavy alcohol use is relatively more common among people living in small metropolitan areas than in large metropolitan areas and nonmetropolitan areas and is highest among those living in the North Central region of the United States. Heavy smokers are more likely to live in nonmetropolitan areas and in the North Central or Southern regions. Rates of heavy alcohol use and heavy smoking are highest among those with less than a college degree and less than a high school diploma, respectively.

Indicator 12

Heavy Cigarette Use by Youth Varies by Race and Ethnic Group

Percent of High School Seniors Who Are Heavy Users

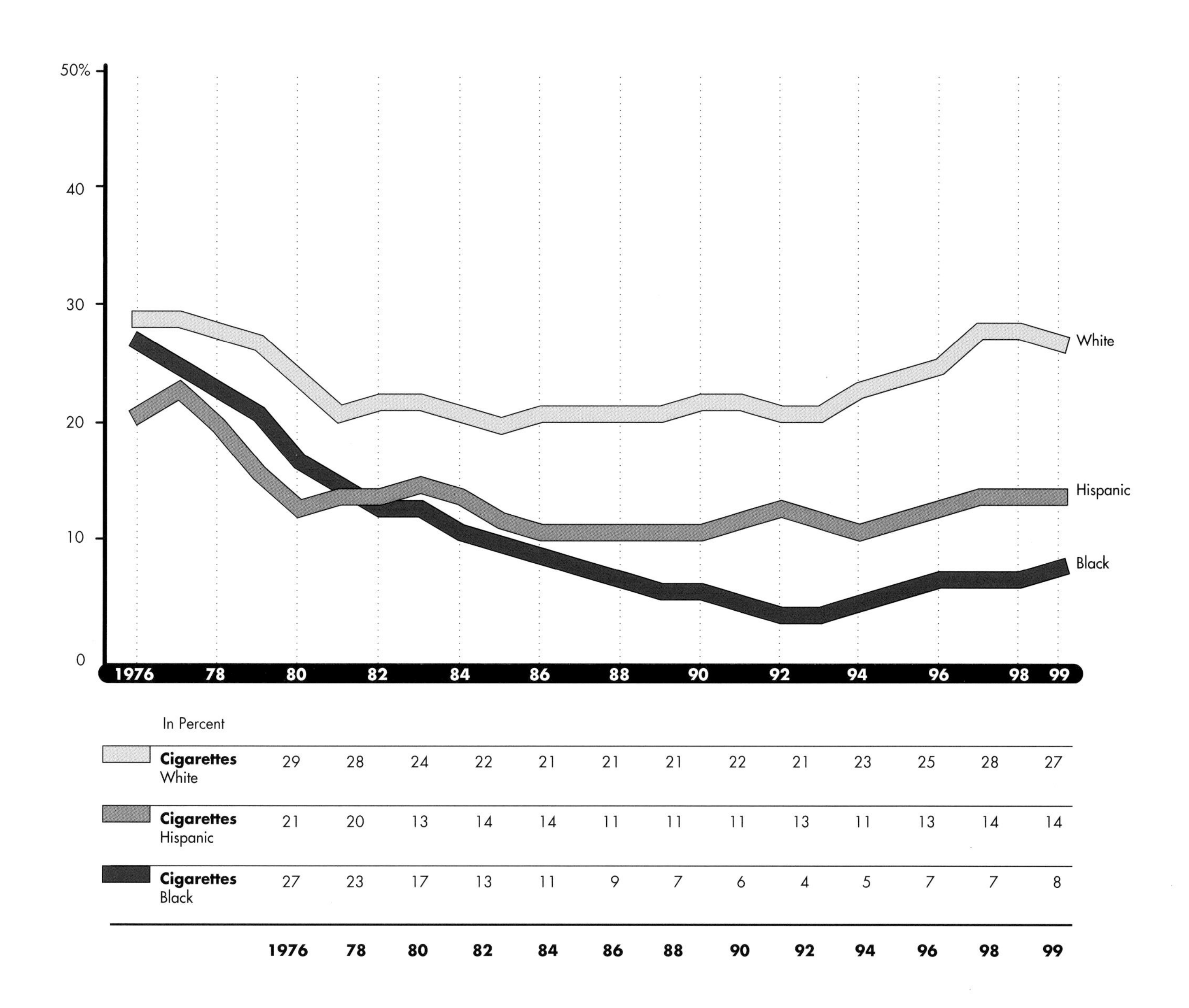

In Percent

	1976	78	80	82	84	86	88	90	92	94	96	98	99
Cigarettes White	29	28	24	22	21	21	21	22	21	23	25	28	27
Cigarettes Hispanic	21	20	13	14	14	11	11	11	13	11	13	14	14
Cigarettes Black	27	23	17	13	11	9	7	6	4	5	7	7	8

NOTES: Each point plotted is the mean of the specified year and the previous year. Hispanic data are derived from self-reports. Heavy tobacco use is daily use in the past 30 days.

SOURCE: Johnston LD, O'Malley PM, Bachman JG. *National Survey Results on Drug Use from the Monitoring the Future Study, 1975–1999. Volume I: Secondary School Students.* Rockville, MD: National Institute on Drug Abuse, 2000. Table D–49, p. 464.

Attempts to Quit

Many people who smoke, drink or use drugs have experienced some kind of problem related to use and have tried to stop. Because quitting is hard, relapse rates are high, and some people have to try a number of times before they are successful. Indeed, addiction is frequently a chronic, relapsing health condition for many people.

Some users of alcohol, tobacco and illicit drugs become dependent or addicted. People who are dependent on a drug may experience one or more of the following potential signs of dependence: wanting or trying to decrease substance use; increasing tolerance and the need for greater amounts to achieve the same effect; spending significant time getting, using or withdrawing from drug use in the past month; using the drug more often or in larger amounts than intended; use of the drug interfering with important daily activities; and/or use of the drug resulting in emotional, psychological or health problems.

Cigarettes are most likely to result in dependence, and 60 percent of those who smoked in the past year, and 77 percent of those who smoke a pack or more a day, reported having at least one of the symptoms of dependence. Among individuals reporting past year use, 42 percent of those who had used marijuana reported at least one of these symptoms, followed by 38 percent of those who had used cocaine and 23 percent of those who had used alcohol (Indicator 13).

To break the smoking habit, many people try to quit or cut back. It is estimated that 68 percent of current smokers want to quit, and about 46 percent have tried to quit in the past year. Quitting smoking is difficult, however, and more than half of those who smoked a pack or more a day reported failure in trying to quit or even cut back. The typical smoker who becomes a confirmed former smoker usually makes at least two or three attempts, or more, before quitting successfully.

More than 44 million adults have quit smoking, and almost half of all adults in the United States who ever smoked have quit. The percentage of smokers who quit increased dramatically after the release of the 1964 Surgeon General's report documenting the negative health effects of smoking (Indicator 14). Indeed, concern about health is mentioned by nine out of ten smokers as the reason they attempted to stop smoking.

Indicator 13

Smokers Are More Likely to Report Dependence Symptoms than Users of Other Substances, 1998

Percent of Past Year Users Reporting Symptoms of Dependence

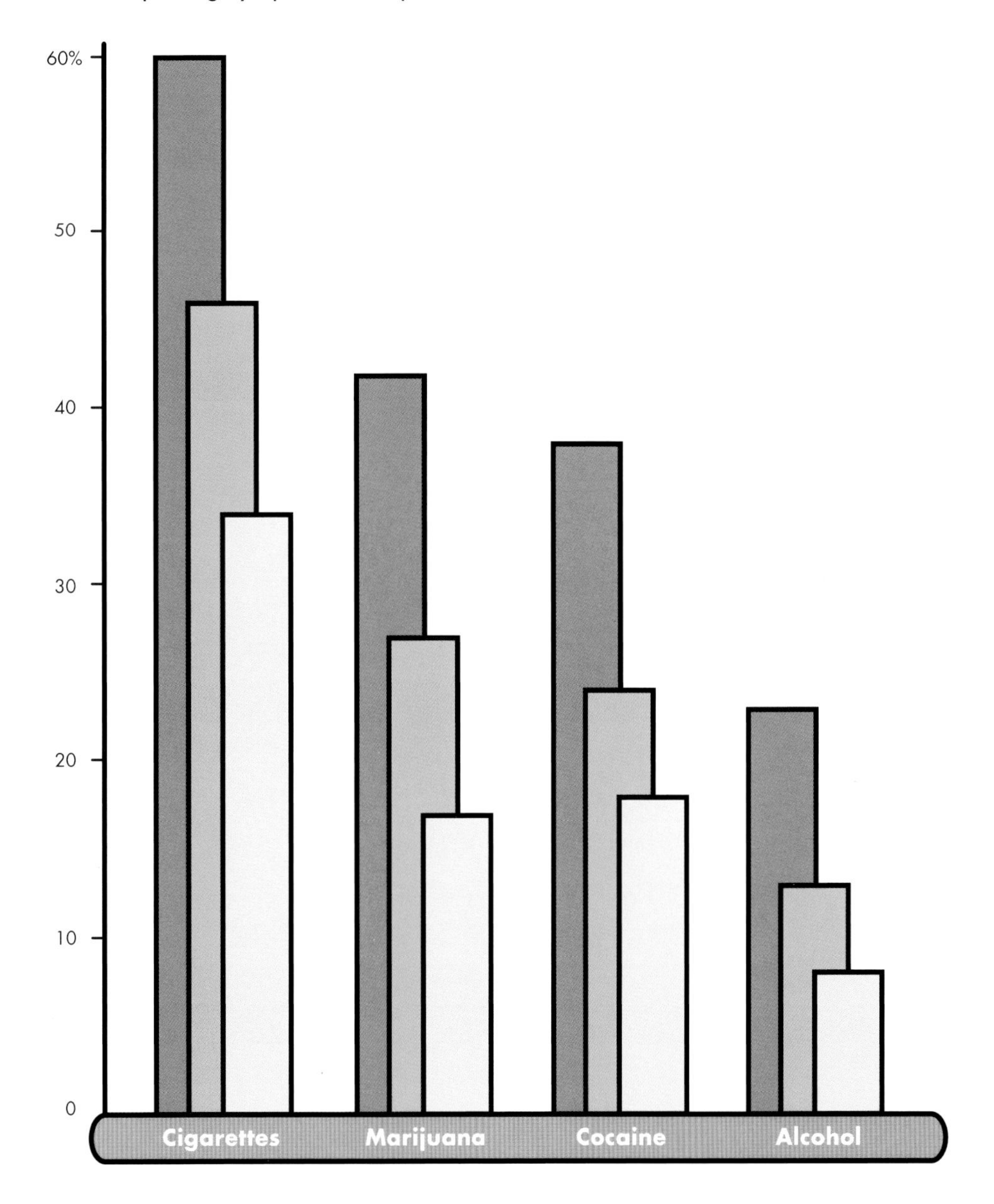

In Percent

	Cigarettes	Marijuana	Cocaine	Alcohol
1 symptom	60	42	38	23
2 symptoms	46	27	24	13
3 or more symptoms	34	17	18	8

NOTES: Individuals were asked if they had in the past year experienced any of seven behavioral or psychological problems that are potentially and cumulatively indicative of drug dependence. Past year use includes those who had used at least once in the past year.

SOURCE: U.S. Substance Abuse and Mental Health Services Administration, Office of Applied Studies. *National Household Survey on Drug Abuse Main Findings, 1998.* Rockville, MD, 2000. pp. 136–139.

Attempts to Quit (continued)

Interest in quitting is highest in women, middle-aged smokers and those with 12 to 15 years of education, and it is lowest among older persons and those with lower levels of education and income. The percentage of people who ever smoked and who are now former smokers is higher among the elderly than other age groups, among men than women, among whites than blacks and among college graduates than those with less education. Despite the increase in the percentage of adults who have quit, about 51 million Americans—47 million adults and 4 million youths—are current smokers, defined as those who had smoked in the past 30 days.

In 1997, among those who had used any alcohol in the past year, 7 percent reported that they wanted or tried to decrease their use but could not. Heavier drinkers had even more difficulty in their attempts to quit or curtail use. Among those who had five or more drinks on each of five or more occasions in the past 30 days, 21 percent reported an inability to decrease use.

In 1997, 17 percent of those who had used marijuana on 12 or more days in the past year reported that they wanted or tried to decrease their use but could not. For young adults, predictors of marijuana cessation include prior degree of involvement with legal and illegal drugs, pregnancy and parenthood for women, frequency of use and age at first use. For cocaine, 30 percent who had used cocaine on 12 or more days in the past year reported that they wanted or tried to decrease their use but could not.

Indicator 14

More than 44 Million Adults Are Former Smokers; 47 Million Are Current Smokers

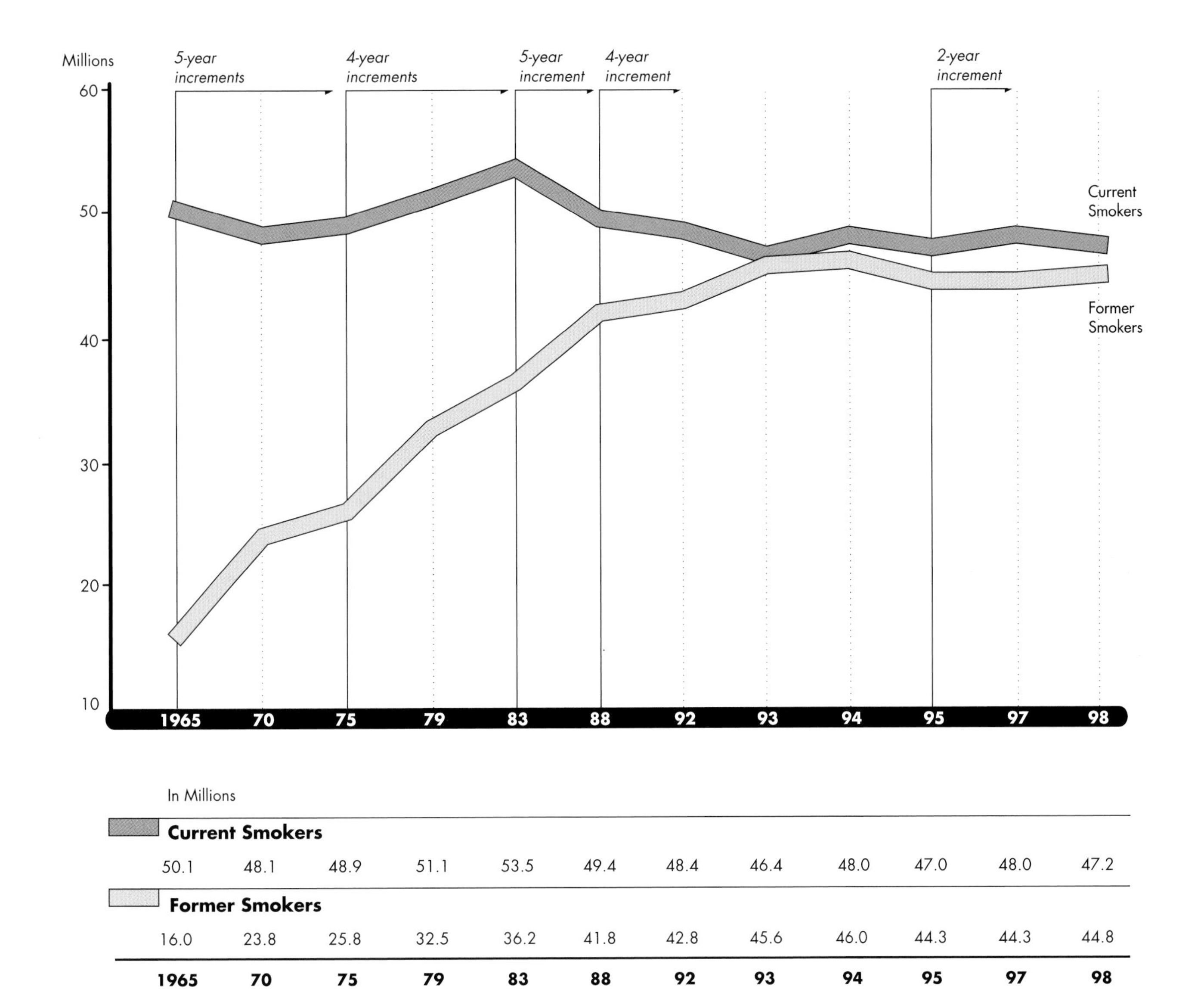

In Millions

	1965	70	75	79	83	88	92	93	94	95	97	98
Current Smokers	50.1	48.1	48.9	51.1	53.5	49.4	48.4	46.4	48.0	47.0	48.0	47.2
Former Smokers	16.0	23.8	25.8	32.5	36.2	41.8	42.8	45.6	46.0	44.3	44.3	44.8

SOURCES: For 1965–1995: U.S. Centers for Disease Control and Prevention. Tobacco Information and Prevention Sourcepage: Cessation. Number of Adults 18 Years and Older Who Were Current, Former or Never Smokers, Overall and by Sex, Race, Hispanic Origin, Age and Education. National Health Interview Surveys, Selected Years—United States, 1965–1995. www.cdc.gov/tobacco

For 1997: U.S. Centers for Disease Control and Prevention. "Cigarette Smoking Among Adults—United States, 1997," *Morbidity and Mortality Weekly Report* 48(43): 993–936, November 1999. For 1998: U.S. Centers for Disease Control and Prevention. "Cigarette Smoking Among Adults—United States, 1998." *Morbidity and Mortality Weekly Report*, 49 (39): 881–884, October 2000.

Section I

Patterns of Use

GENERAL

Anthony JC, Warner LA and Kessler RC. "Comparative Epidemiology of Dependence on Tobacco, Alcohol, Controlled Substances, and Inhalants: Basic Findings from the National Comorbidity Survey." *Experimental and Clinical Psychopharmacology*, 2(3): 244–268, 1994.

Grant BF. "Prevalence and Correlates of Alcohol Use and DSM-IV Alcohol Dependence in the United States: Results of the National Longitudinal Alcohol Epidemiologic Survey." *Journal of Studies on Alcohol,* 58(5): 464–473, 1997.

Johnston LD, O'Malley PM and Bachman JG. *National Survey Results on Drug Use from the Monitoring the Future Study, 1975–1999. Volume I: Secondary School Students.* Rockville, MD: National Institute on Drug Abuse, 2000.

Johnston LD, O'Malley PM and Bachman JG. *National Survey Results on Drug Use from the Monitoring the Future Study, 1975–1999. Volume II: College Students and Young Adults.* Rockville, MD: National Institute on Drug Abuse, 2000.

National Institute on Alcohol Abuse and Alcoholism. *Tenth Special Report to the U.S. Congress on Alcohol and Health from the Secretary of Health and Human Services.* Rockville, MD, 2000.

U.S. Substance Abuse and Mental Health Services Administration, Office of Applied Studies. *Summary of Findings from the 1999 National Household Survey on Drug Abuse.* Rockville, MD, 2000.

PERCEPTION OF RISK

Bachman JG, Johnston LD and O'Malley PM. "Explaining the Recent Increases in Students' Marijuana Use: The Impacts of Perceived Risks and Disapproval from 1976 through 1996." *American Journal of Public Health*, 88:887–892, 1998.

The University of Michigan News and Information Services, Press Release of the *Monitoring the Future Study*, "Ecstasy Use Rises Sharply Among Teens in 2000; Use of Many Other Drugs Stays Steady, but Significant Declines Are Reported for Some," December 13, 2000.

IMPLICATIONS OF EARLY USE

Califano J and Luntz F. "Back to School 1998—The CASA National Survey of American Attitudes on Substance Abuse IV: Teens, Teachers and Principals," The National Center on Addiction and Substance Abuse at Columbia University, New York, NY, 1998.

Chen K and Kandel DB. "The Natural History of Drug Use from Adolescence to the Mid-Thirties in a General Population Sample." *American Journal of Public Health*, 85(1): 41–47, 1995.

O'Malley PM, Johnston LD and Bachman JG. "Alcohol Use among Adolescents." *Alcohol Health & Research World*, 22:85–93, 1998.

TRENDS IN USE

Wechsler H, Lee J, Kuo M and Lee H. "College Binge Drinking in the 1990s: A Continuing Problem: Results of the Harvard School of Public Health 1999 College Alcohol Study," *The Journal of American College Health*, Vol. 48, p. 199–210, March 2000.

DEMOGRAPHIC DIFFERENCES IN HEAVY USE

Kessler RC, Crum RM, Warner LA, Nelson CB, Schulenberg J and Anthony JC. "Lifetime Co-occurrence of DSM-III-R Alcohol Abuse and Dependence with Other Psychiatric Disorders in the National Comorbidity Survey." *Archives of General Psychiatry*, 54(4): 313–321, 1997.

U.S. Department of Health and Human Services. *Tobacco Use among U.S. Racial/Ethnic Minority Groups—African Americans, American Indians and Alaska Natives, Asian Americans and Pacific Islanders, and Hispanics: A Report of the Surgeon General.* Atlanta, GA: U.S. Department of Health and Human Services, Centers for Disease Control and Prevention, National Center for Chronic Disease Prevention and Health Promotion, Office on Smoking and Health, 1998.

U.S. Substance Abuse and Mental Health Services Administration, Office of Applied Studies. *Prevalence of Substance Use among Racial and Ethnic Subgroups in the United States 1991–1993.* Rockville, MD, 1998.

U.S. Substance Abuse and Mental Health Services Administration, Office of Applied Studies. *Substance Use among Women in the United States.* Rockville, MD, 1997.

ATTEMPTS TO QUIT

Orleans CT and Cummings KM. "Population-based tobacco control: Progress and prospects." *American Journal of Health Promotion*, 14(2): 83–91, Nov.–Dec. 1999.

U.S. Centers for Disease Control and Prevention. "Cigarette Smoking Among Adults—United States, 1998." *Morbidity and Mortality Weekly Report*, 49(39): 881–884, 2000.

Consequences of Use

- Each year, more than five million years of life could have been saved if every person who died that year from cigarette smoking had lived to his or her average life expectancy.
- More than 100,000 deaths in the United States each year are attributable to excessive alcohol consumption. Causes directly or indirectly related to alcohol deaths include drunk driving, cancer, stroke, cirrhosis of the liver, falls and other adverse effects.
- More than one-third of all AIDS deaths in the United States have occurred among injecting drug users and their sexual partners. AIDS among this group is a major cause of illicit drug-related deaths, with a disproportionate impact on minority Americans.
- Substance abuse drives up health care costs. In 1995, health care spending associated with alcohol, tobacco and drug abuse was estimated at more than $114 billion. Smoking accounted for 70 percent of these costs.
- Among adult current drinkers, more than half say they have a blood relative who is or was an alcoholic or problem drinker.
- At least half of adults arrested for major crimes—including homicide, theft and assault—tested positive for drugs at the time of their arrest. Among those convicted of violent crimes, approximately half of state prison inmates and 40 percent of federal prisoners had been drinking or taking drugs at the time of their offense.
- Among full-time workers, heavy drinkers and illicit drug users are more likely than those who do not drink heavily or use illicit drugs to have skipped work in the past month or have worked for three or more employers in the past year.

Tobacco Deaths

Between 1990 and 1994, cigarette smoking accounted for 2.2 million deaths—an average of 430,700 deaths a year, or 20 percent of all U.S. deaths (Indicator 15). If current smoking patterns continue, an estimated 25 million people alive today, including five million people currently under age 18, will die prematurely of a smoking-related disease. Each year, more than five million years of life could be saved if every person who died that year from cigarette smoking had lived to his or her average life expectancy.

Cigarette smoking has long been known to cause cancer, and nearly 90 percent of lung cancer deaths result from smoking. Lung cancer death rates, always high among men—especially blacks—peaked in 1990 and have since declined 9 percent (Indicator 16). Rates for women are much lower than those for men, but they continue to rise, although at a slower pace since 1990. Lung cancer death rates among women rose 5 percent between 1990 and 1995, with a smaller increase among black women. A major reason for the gender difference in lung cancer death rates is that lung cancer mortality trends reflect smoking trends, and the increase in smoking occurred later for women, rising in the 1960s, while smoking rates fell for men during this period. Lung cancer deaths surpass deaths from all other kinds of cancer—exceeding prostate cancer in men and breast cancer in women.

Lung cancer also accounts for the vast majority of cancer deaths related to cigarette smoking, and it is the leading cause of all deaths attributable to smoking each year. Even so, lung cancer accounts for only slightly more than a quarter (28 percent) of all deaths attributed to smoking. Smoking also contributes to deaths from coronary heart disease, chronic bronchitis and emphysema, stroke, other cancers, including cancers of the pancreas, trachea, bronchus and larynx, and a variety of other illnesses.

Most deaths associated with smoking occur among the smokers themselves, but exposure to environmental tobacco smoke also is an acknowledged health hazard that each year results in an estimated 3,000 lung cancer deaths among nonsmokers. In addition, more than 6,000 deaths among children each year are linked in part to parental smoking, primarily from low birthweights related to

Indicator 15

More than 430,000 Smoking-Related Deaths Occur Annually

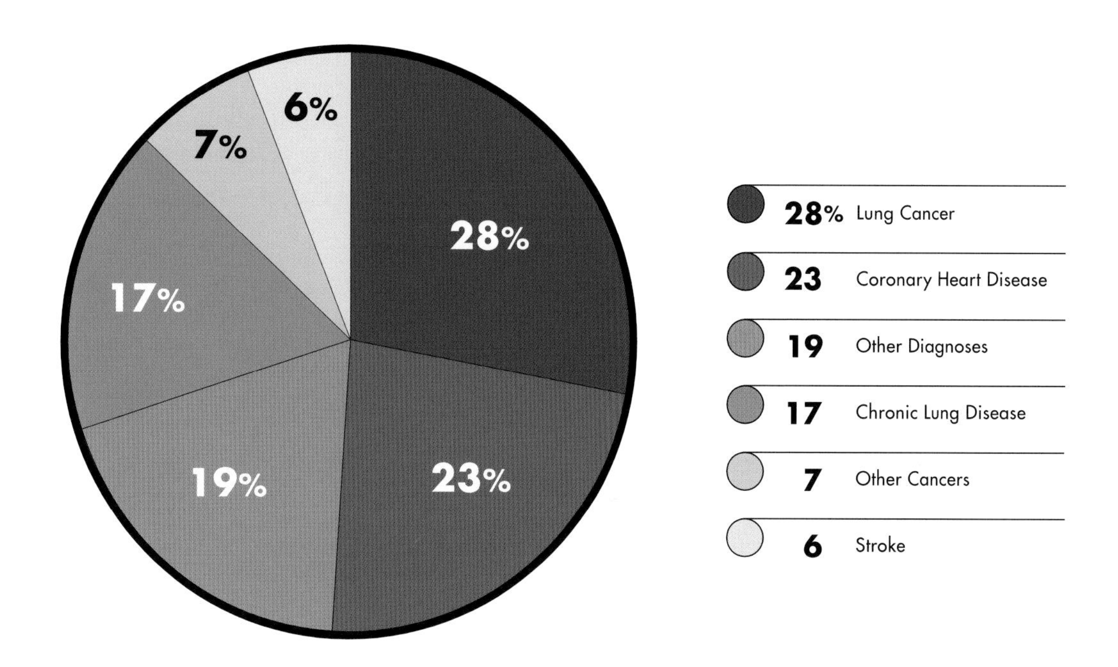

NOTES: Lung cancer and other smoking deaths are estimates of deaths where smoking is an attributable factor, including cardiovascular and cerebrovascular diseases. Number of deaths are annual averages calculated from 1990–1994 estimates.

SOURCES: U.S. Centers for Disease Control and Prevention. "Smoking-Attributable Mortality and Years of Potential Life Lost—United States, 1984." Editorial Note—1997. *Morbidity and Mortality Weekly Report*, 46(20): 444–451, 1997. www.cdc.gov/tobacco/oshaag.htm

smoking during pregnancy or respiratory infections and sudden infant death syndrome associated with parents' smoking. In fact, the Surgeon General has declared smoking the single most important preventable cause of poor pregnancy outcome. In 1996, an estimated 15 million children under age 18 were exposed to tobacco smoke in the home from family members who smoked.

Overall, exposure to environmental tobacco smoke is widespread, and almost 90 percent of nonsmokers age 4 years and older are exposed to some tobacco smoke. Since the mid- to late 1980s, the percentage of schools, workplaces and public places with policies banning or limiting smoking has increased, and second-hand smoke exposure is expected to decline.

Indicator 16

Lung Cancer Deaths Higher for Males but Declining

Age-Adjusted Lung Cancer Deaths per 100,000 People

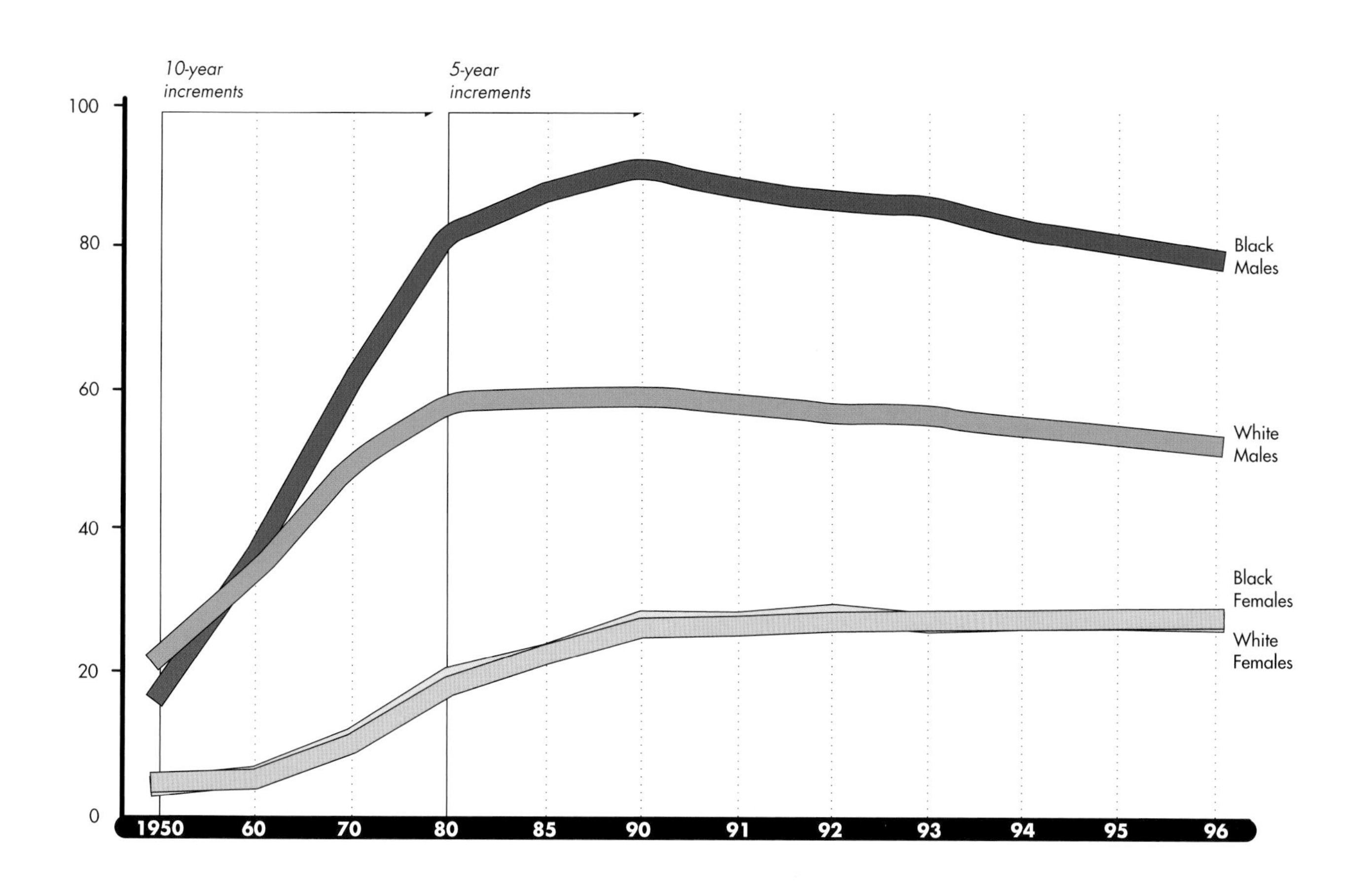

Per 100,000 People	1950	60	70	80	85	90	91	92	93	94	95	96
Black Males	16.9	36.6	60.8	82.0	87.7	91.0	88.4	86.7	86.0	82.8	80.5	78.5
White Males	21.6	34.6	49.9	58.0	58.7	59.0	58.1	56.7	56.3	54.8	53.7	52.6
Black Females	4.1	5.5	10.9	19.5	22.8	27.5	27.4	28.5	27.3	27.7	27.8	27.6
White Females	4.6	5.1	10.1	18.2	22.7	26.5	26.8	27.4	27.6	27.7	27.9	28.0

NOTES: Lung cancers and other smoking deaths are estimates of deaths where smoking is an attributable factor, including cardiovascular and cerebrovascular diseases. Lung cancer refers to all respiratory cancers. Although use rates for different substances vary by ethnicity, death rates are consistently higher for blacks than whites.

SOURCES: For 1991–1992: National Center for Health Statistics. *Health United States 1994.* Hyattsville, MD, 1995. For other years: National Center for Health Statistics. *Health United States 1998 with Socioeconomic Status and Health Chartbook.* Hyattsville, MD, 1998.

Alcohol Deaths

Alcohol abuse is a major cause of premature death and illness in the United States. More than 100,000 deaths each year in the United States are attributable to excessive alcohol consumption (Indicator 17). Although there may be potential health benefits of light to moderate drinking for men and women, including those older than age 65, on average, people dying from alcohol-related causes lose 26 years from their normal life expectancy. Heavy drinking contributes to illness in each of the top three causes of death: heart disease, cancer and stroke. Overall alcohol mortality rates are particularly high among black men, even though alcohol use tends to be more moderate for blacks than whites and Hispanics (Indicator 18).

Cirrhosis of the liver and alcohol-related motor vehicle fatalities are considered important annual indicators of alcohol-related mortality trends. Compared to the total population, cirrhosis death rates are higher for blacks, Hispanics, American Indians and Alaskan Natives. The alcohol-related motor vehicle fatality rate is also particularly high, compared to the total population, for American Indians and Alaskan Natives.

The tenth leading cause of death—liver disease—is largely preventable, because nearly half of all cirrhosis deaths are linked to alcohol. Cirrhosis deaths are a marker of long-term alcohol use and, accordingly, are more prevalent among people in middle age and older. Since 1970, death rates for alcohol-related liver cirrhosis have dropped 26 percent.

Alcohol-related motor vehicle fatalities also continue to decline (see table). Between 1987 and 1997, the number of alcohol-related traffic fatalities dropped 32 percent, and intoxication rates for drivers involved in fatal crashes decreased for all age groups—especially among young drivers age 16 to 20. Still, traffic crashes remain the single greatest cause of death among America's youth and young adults.

The recent decline in alcohol-related traffic fatalities may be due, in part, to declines in both chronic and inappropriate use among even casual drinkers, particularly young people. Federal requirements to restrict access to alcohol for those under age 21, and legislation in some states to lower the allowable blood alcohol concentration for young

Indicator 17

Alcohol-Related Deaths Top 110,000 in 1996

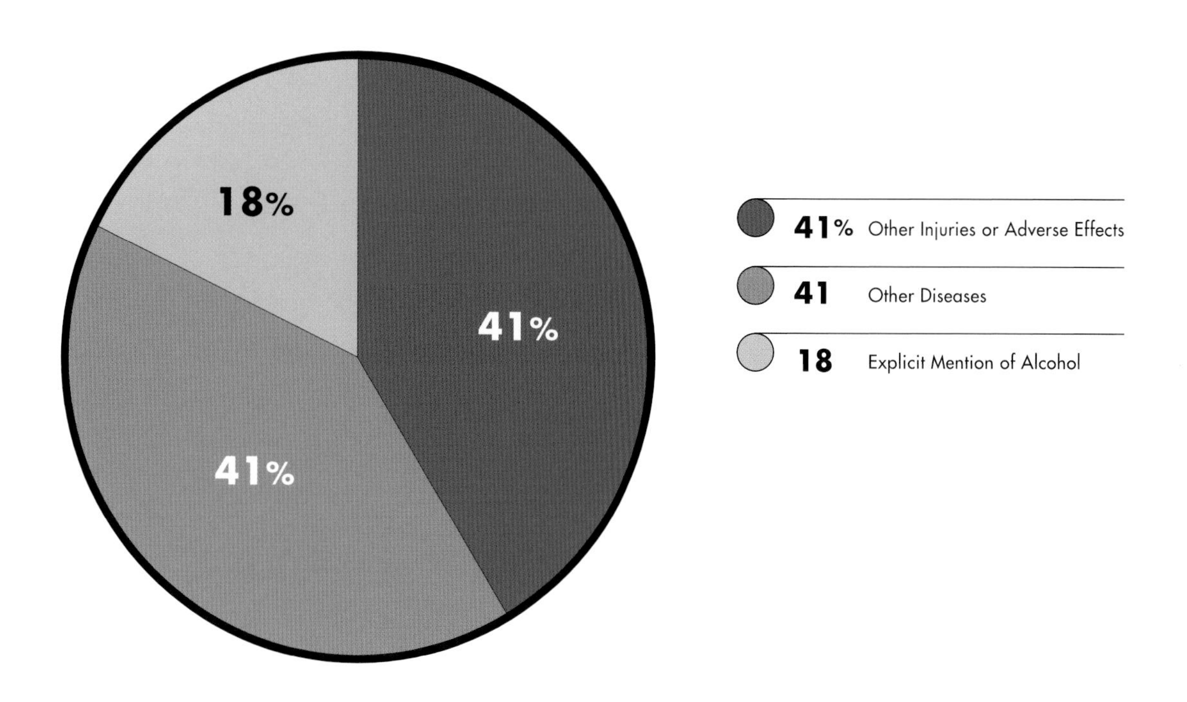

NOTES: Causes of death from other alcohol-related injuries or adverse effects refer to where some of the deaths are alcohol-related (e.g., motor vehicle accidents, homicide). Causes of death from other alcohol-related diseases refer to where some of the deaths are alcohol-related (e.g., malignant neoplasm of the stomach, chronic pancreatitis). Causes of death with explicit mention of alcohol refer to deaths that are all alcohol-related (e.g., alcoholic cirrhosis of the liver, accidental poisoning by alcohol).

SOURCE: Unpublished Alcohol Epidemiologic Data System data. National Institute on Alcohol Abuse and Alcoholism. Quick Fact Data Table: "Number of deaths and age-adjusted death rates per 100,000 population for categories of alcohol-related (A-R) mortality, United States and States, 1979–96." www.silk.nih.gov/silk/niaaa1/database/armort01.txt

Deaths from Alcohol-Related Traffic Injuries Continue to Decline

	Alcohol-Related Traffic Fatalities		Total Number of Traffic Fatalities
Year	Number	Percent	
1982	25,165	57%	43,945
1983	23,646	56	42,589
1984	23,758	54	44,257
1985	22,716	52	43,825
1986	24,045	52	46,087
1987	23,641	51	46,390
1988	23,626	50	47,087
1989	22,404	49	45,582
1990	22,084	50	44,599
1991	19,887	48	41,508
1992	17,858	46	39,250
1993	17,473	44	40,150
1994	16,580	41	40,716
1995	17,247	41	41,817
1996	17,126	41	42,065
1997	16,189	39	42,013
1998	15,935	38	41,501
1999	15,786	38	41,611

NOTES: Traffic fatalities are number of deaths from crashes in which at least one person dies within 30 days of the crash. The National Highway Traffic Safety Administration defines a fatality or fatal crash as alcohol-related if either a driver or nonmotorist (usually a pedestrian) has a blood alcohol concentration of 0.01% or above.

SOURCES: U.S. Department of Transportation, National Highway Traffic Safety Administration. *Traffic Safety Facts 1996: A Compilation of Motor Vehicle Crash Data from the Fatality Analysis Reporting System and the General Estimates System.* Washington, DC, 1997. U.S. Department of Transportation, National Highway Traffic Safety Administration. *Traffic Safety Facts 1997: Alcohol.* Washington, DC, 1998. U.S. Department of Transportation, National Highway Traffic Safety Administration. *Traffic Safety Facts 1998: Alcohol.* Washington, DC, 1999. U.S. Department of Transportation, National Highway Traffic Safety Administration. *Traffic Safety Facts 1999:* Alcohol. Washington, DC, 2000

people, may also contribute to the decline. Diverse efforts underway in communities across the country—including prompt license suspension, sobriety police checks, zero tolerance for underage drivers and public education such as designated driver programs—also may have had an impact on alcohol-impaired driving.

Evidence links a high proportion of deaths from falls, fires and burns and drownings to drinking. After motor vehicle injury deaths, falls are the second leading cause of all unintentional fatal injuries in the United States, drownings the fourth and fires and burns the sixth. Various studies estimate that between 13 percent and 63 percent of falls are alcohol-related, and between 33 percent and 61 percent of people who die in fires had been drinking. One common cause of fire among intoxicated people is falling asleep or passing out before extinguishing a cigarette. Alcohol use is also implicated in one-third of drownings.

Indicator 18

Deaths from Alcohol Use Highest for Black Males, though White Males More Likely to Drink

Age-Adjusted Alcohol-Related Deaths per 100,000 People

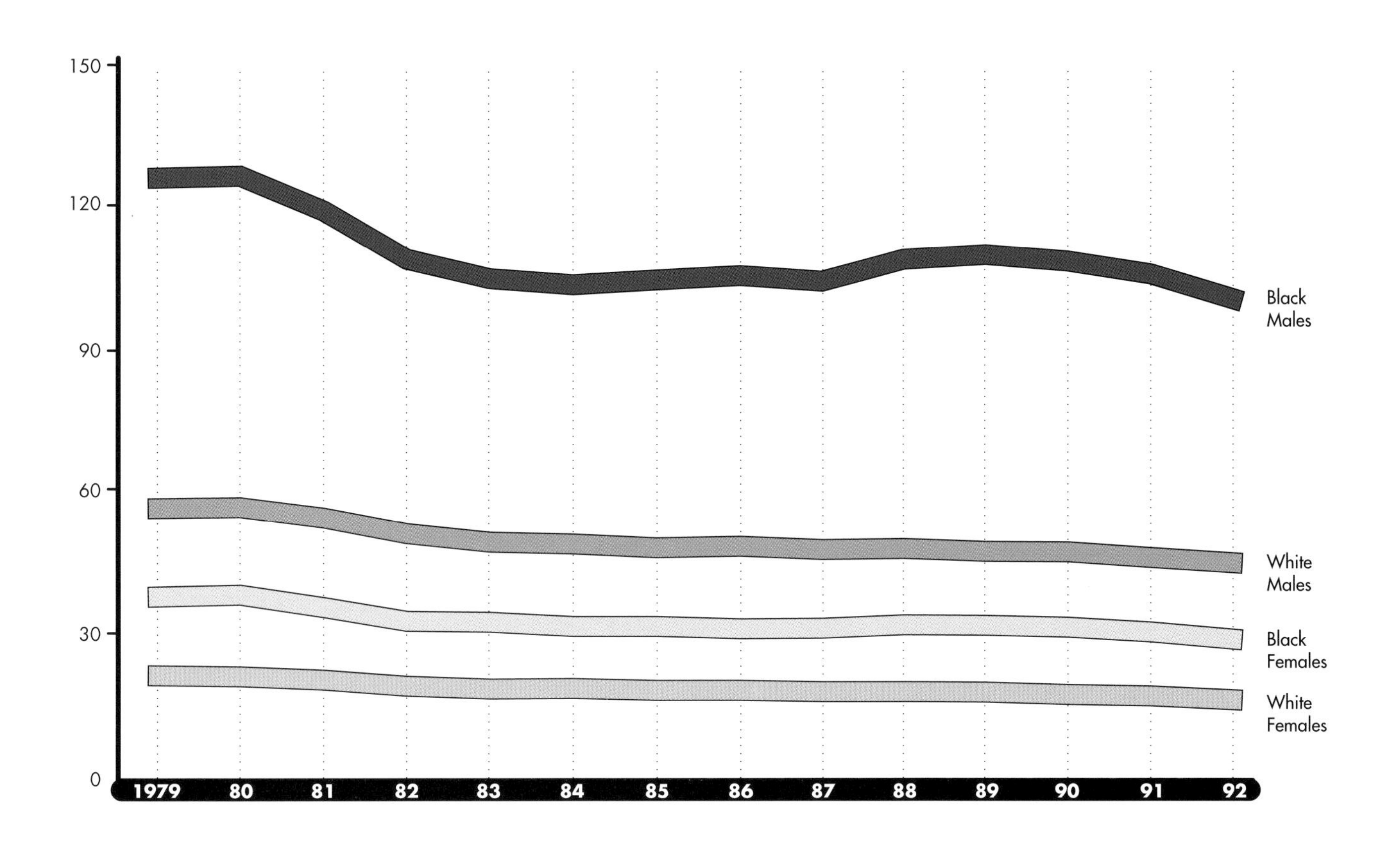

Per 100,000 People

	1979	80	81	82	83	84	85	86	87	88	89	90	91	92
Black Males	126.1	126.5	119.2	109.0	104.9	103.6	104.6	105.5	104.3	108.9	109.9	108.5	105.8	100.6
White Males	56.6	56.8	54.6	51.3	49.5	49.1	48.3	48.6	47.9	48.1	47.5	47.4	46.2	45.1
Black Females	38.0	38.4	35.8	32.9	32.7	31.8	31.8	31.3	31.4	32.1	32 .0	31.6	30.6	29.1
White Females	21.4	21.2	20.5	19.2	18.6	18.7	18.3	18.3	18.0	18.0	17.9	17.4	17.1	16.3

NOTES: Includes deaths directly and indirectly related to alcohol use. Although use rates for different substances vary by ethnicity, death rates are consistently higher for blacks than whites.

SOURCE: Stinson FS, Nephew TM. "State Trends in Alcohol-Related Mortality, 1979–92." *U.S. Alcohol Epidemiologic Data Reference Manual, Vol. 5.* Bethesda, MD: National Institute on Alcohol Abuse and Alcoholism, 1996.

Illicit Drug Deaths

Drug-related deaths have more than doubled since the early 1980s (Indicator 19). Deaths related to drugs often involve a lethal combination of two or more illicit drugs or drugs combined with alcohol. Heroin or cocaine is involved in 70 percent of drug deaths. The number of people dying from conditions directly identified with illicit drugs—for example, overdose—is smaller than the number of deaths from conditions directly identified with alcohol, but the gap has narrowed in recent years.

Reported deaths directly related to drugs grossly underestimate the mortality toll from illicit drugs. This is because they exclude deaths from associated diseases, such as AIDS among injecting drug users, hepatitis and tuberculosis, and from other indirect causes of death, such as homicides, falls and motor vehicle crashes. One recent study estimated 25,493 deaths attributable to drug abuse in 1992, including deaths related to AIDS, hepatitis, tuberculosis, homicides and injuries. Medical examiner data from 1996 indicate that about one-third of drug deaths involve illicit drugs as a contributing factor, but not as the direct cause of death. Approximately one in five drug deaths is a suicide.

Nearly 40 percent of directly related illicit drug deaths are among adults between age 35 and 44. Those 25 and younger accounted for another 10 percent of illicit drug deaths. Overall, rates are higher for males than for females, and for blacks than for whites (Indicator 20). Black males are 1.7 times as likely as white males, and black females are 1.3 times as likely as white females to die from the direct effects of illicit drug use. Between 1987 and 1997, the rate for white males rose the most steeply—77 percent. In contrast, there was a 12 percent increase for black males. Similarly, while there was a 32 percent rise for white females, the rates among black females rose by only 7 percent.

A leading cause of all illicit drug-related deaths is AIDS. By mid-1997, 35 percent of all AIDS deaths that had been reported to the U.S. Centers for Disease Control and Prevention (CDC) were linked to drug abuse. It is encouraging to note that from 1996 to 1997, AIDS deaths among injecting drug users (excluding sex partners) declined 45 percent among men and 33 percent among women.

Nevertheless, the news is not all good. Thirty-two percent of newly diagnosed AIDS cases in the United States occur among

Indicator 19

Deaths Directly Related to Drug Use Have More than Doubled since Early '80s; Deaths Directly Related to Alcohol More Stable

Number of Deaths per Year in Thousands

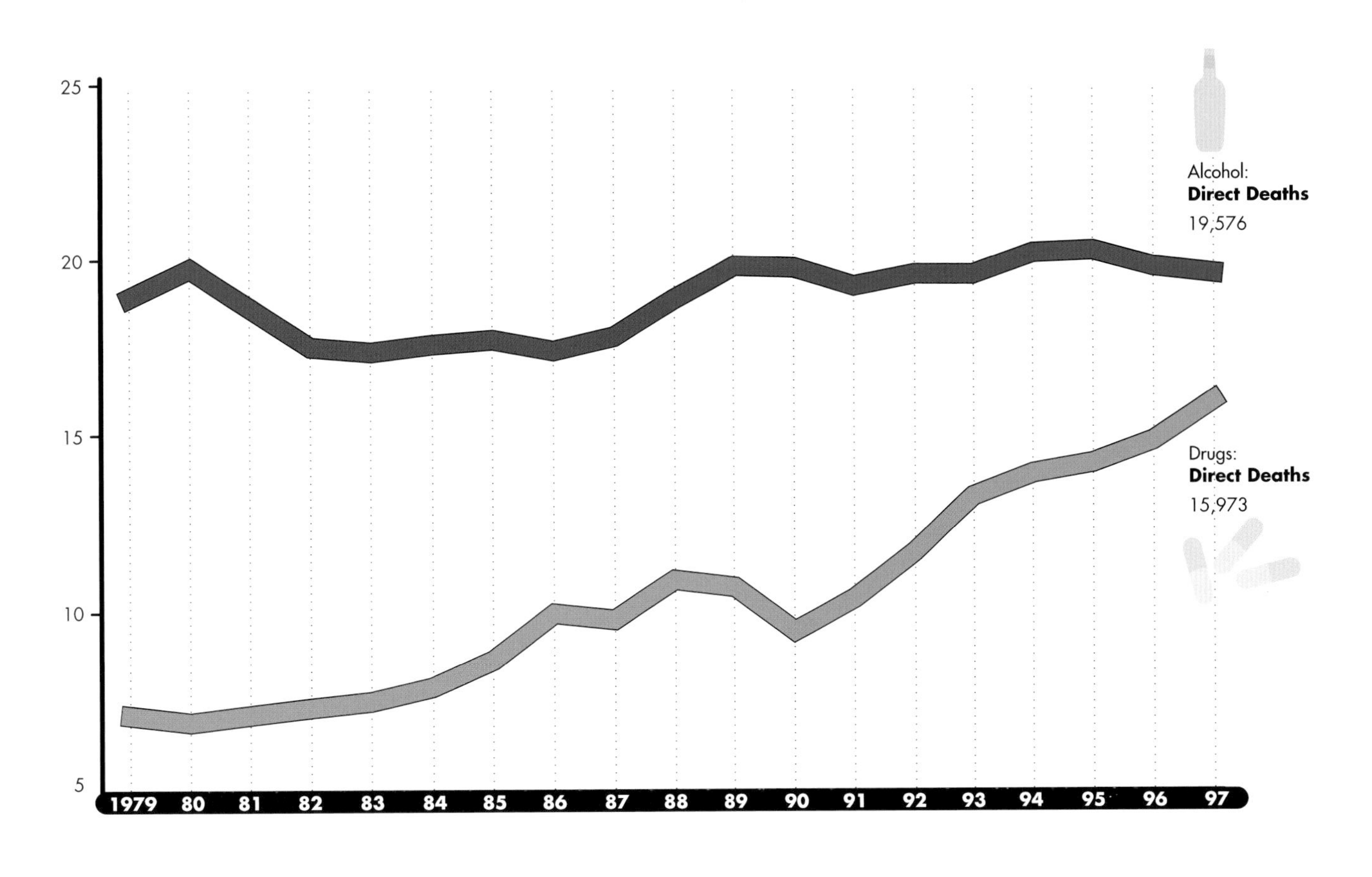

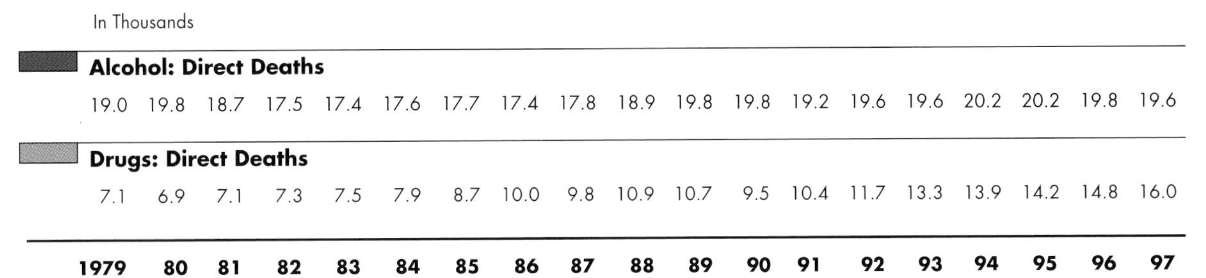

In Thousands

	1979	80	81	82	83	84	85	86	87	88	89	90	91	92	93	94	95	96	97
Alcohol: Direct Deaths	19.0	19.8	18.7	17.5	17.4	17.6	17.7	17.4	17.8	18.9	19.8	19.8	19.2	19.6	19.6	20.2	20.2	19.8	19.6
Drugs: Direct Deaths	7.1	6.9	7.1	7.3	7.5	7.9	8.7	10.0	9.8	10.9	10.7	9.5	10.4	11.7	13.3	13.9	14.2	14.8	16.0

NOTES: Alcohol-direct and drug-direct deaths are conservative because they exclude accidents, homicides and other causes related to alcohol or illicit drug use, but not directly caused by them. AIDS deaths associated with illicit drug abuse are not included in this chart.

SOURCE: Hoyert DL, Kochanek KD, Murphy SL. "Deaths: Final Data for 1997." *National Vital Statistics Report*, 47(19). Hyattsville, MD: National Center for Health Statistics, 1999.

Illicit Drug Deaths (continued)

injecting drug users or people who have had sexual contact with them. Even more troubling, half of all new HIV infection cases occur among injecting drug users (not including their sexual partners), with a disproportionate impact on people in minority groups. HIV/AIDS is having a growing impact on women, largely through injecting drug use or heterosexual contact with injecting drug users. In 1997, 23 percent of AIDS cases occurred among women, up from 7 percent in 1985. Between 1993 and 1997, new HIV cases among women increased 13 percent, but decreased 12 percent for men overall. By 1996, AIDS had become the third leading cause of death among women of reproductive age and the number one cause of death among black women in this age group.

Even nonusers can be victims of a drug-related death—for example, people killed in drug-related violence, drug withdrawal syndrome in newborns or motor vehicle crashes related to illicit drug use. The precise number of these deaths is not known, but they cannot be overlooked in recounting the human toll and significant societal cost of illicit drug abuse.

Indicator 20

Illicit Drug Deaths Increase More for Males than Females in the '90s

Age-Adjusted Deaths Directly Related to Drug Use per 100,000 People

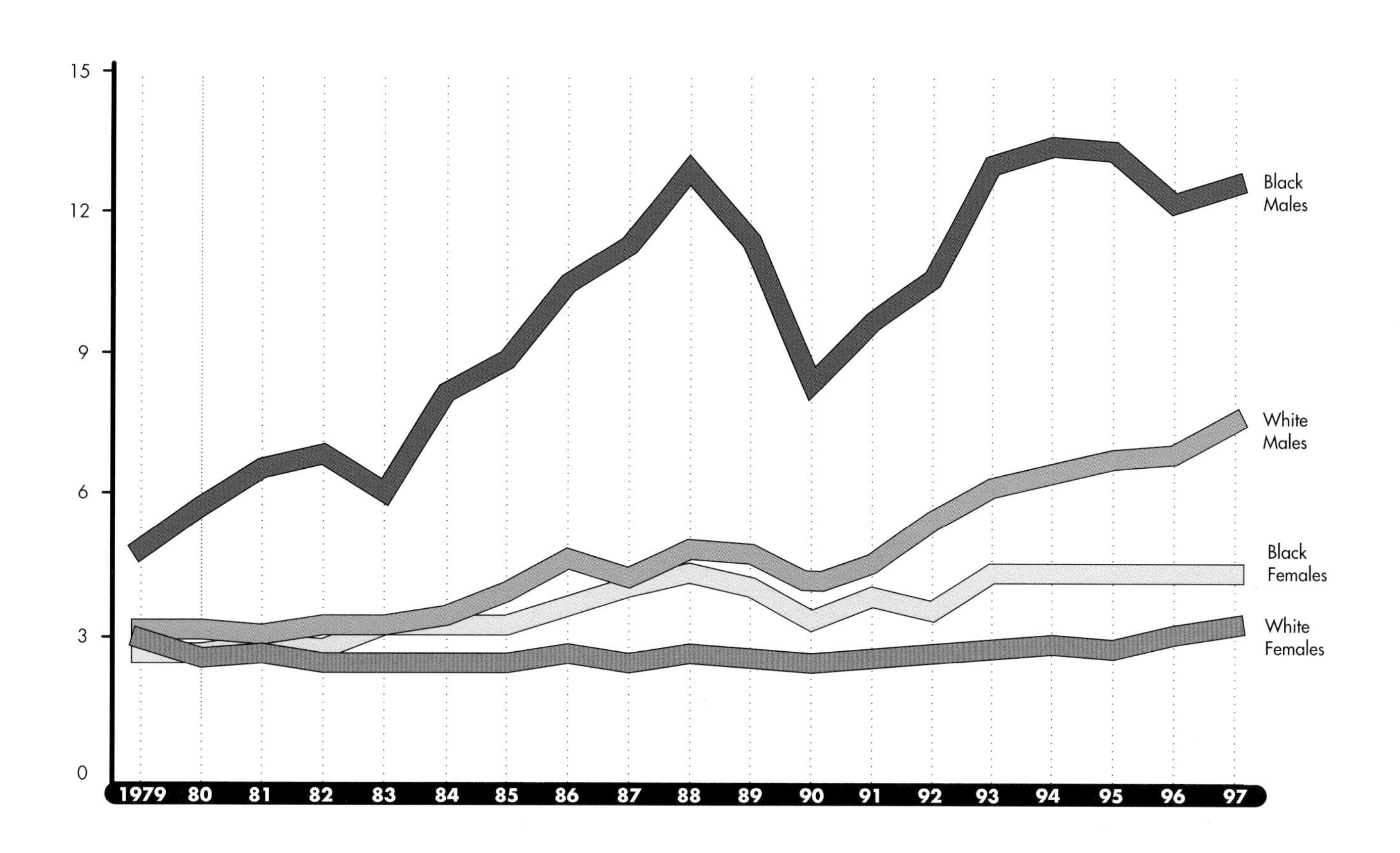

Per 100,000 People

	1979	80	81	82	83	84	85	86	87	88	89	90	91	92	93	94	95	96	97
Black Males	4.9	5.8	6.6	6.9	6.1	8.2	8.9	10.5	11.3	12.9	11.4	8.4	9.7	10.6	13.0	13.4	13.3	12.2	12.6
White Males	3.2	3.2	3.1	3.3	3.3	3.5	4.0	4.7	4.3	4.9	4.8	4.2	4.6	5.5	6.2	6.5	6.8	6.9	7.6
Black Females	2.7	2.7	2.9	2.8	3.3	3.3	3.3	3.7	4.1	4.4	4.1	3.4	3.9	3.6	4.4	4.4	4.4	4.4	4.4
White Females	3.0	2.6	2.7	2.5	2.5	2.5	2.5	2.7	2.5	2.7	2.6	2.5	2.6	2.7	2.8	2.9	2.8	3.1	3.3

NOTE: Although use rates for different substances vary by ethnicity, death rates are consistently higher for blacks than whites.

SOURCE: Hoyert DL, Kochanek KD, Murphy SL. "Deaths: Final Data for 1997." *National Vital Statistics Report*, 47(19). Hyattsville, MD: National Center for Health Statistics, 1999.

Strains on the Nation's Health Care System

Substance abuse adds considerably to the nation's total health care bill. These costs are for treating a host of illnesses and injuries associated with drinking, smoking and using illicit drugs, and include services given in physician's offices, hospitals, emergency rooms (Indicator 21) and substance abuse treatment facilities.

Problem drinkers average four times as many days in the hospital as nondrinkers, mostly because of drinking-related injuries. Likewise, in any given year, smokers use more medical care than people who have never smoked, and when heavy smokers are hospitalized, they stay 25 percent longer than do nonsmokers. Drug users make more than 527,000 visits to costly emergency rooms each year for drug-related problems. Because both alcohol and drug use may result in serious injury, substance users disproportionately need high-cost trauma care. There are also health care costs for people who are not substance users but who are harmed by the behavior of abusers—for example, through motor vehicle crashes. In a study of one inner-city hospital intensive care unit, 21 percent of all admissions were directly alcohol-related.

Tobacco is particularly costly to the nation and overshadows other substances in its impact on health care spending. One of every $14 of the nation's total health care bill is spent on health care for people with smoking-related illnesses. By 1995, smoking-related health care costs were estimated at $80 billion—approximately 70 percent of the health care costs attributed to alcohol, tobacco and illicit drugs combined. This figure did not include health care costs attributable to smoking during pregnancy, environmental tobacco smoke-related illnesses or burn care from smoking-related fires. Health care costs attributed to alcohol abuse in 1995 were nearly twice those of drug abuse-related costs ($23 billion vs. $12 billion).

In addition to hospitals, other providers play a role in substance abusers' care (Indicator 22). For example, many smokers are treated by office physicians, which cost the nation more than $20 billion in 1995; in addition, 12 percent of the medical costs associated with tobacco come from nursing home care for smokers debilitated by chronic health problems. Specialized residential and outpatient treatment centers play an important role in the care and rehabilitation of alco-

Indicator 21

Alcohol and Other Drugs Contribute to Emergency Department Visits

Estimates of Selected Drug Mentions in Thousands

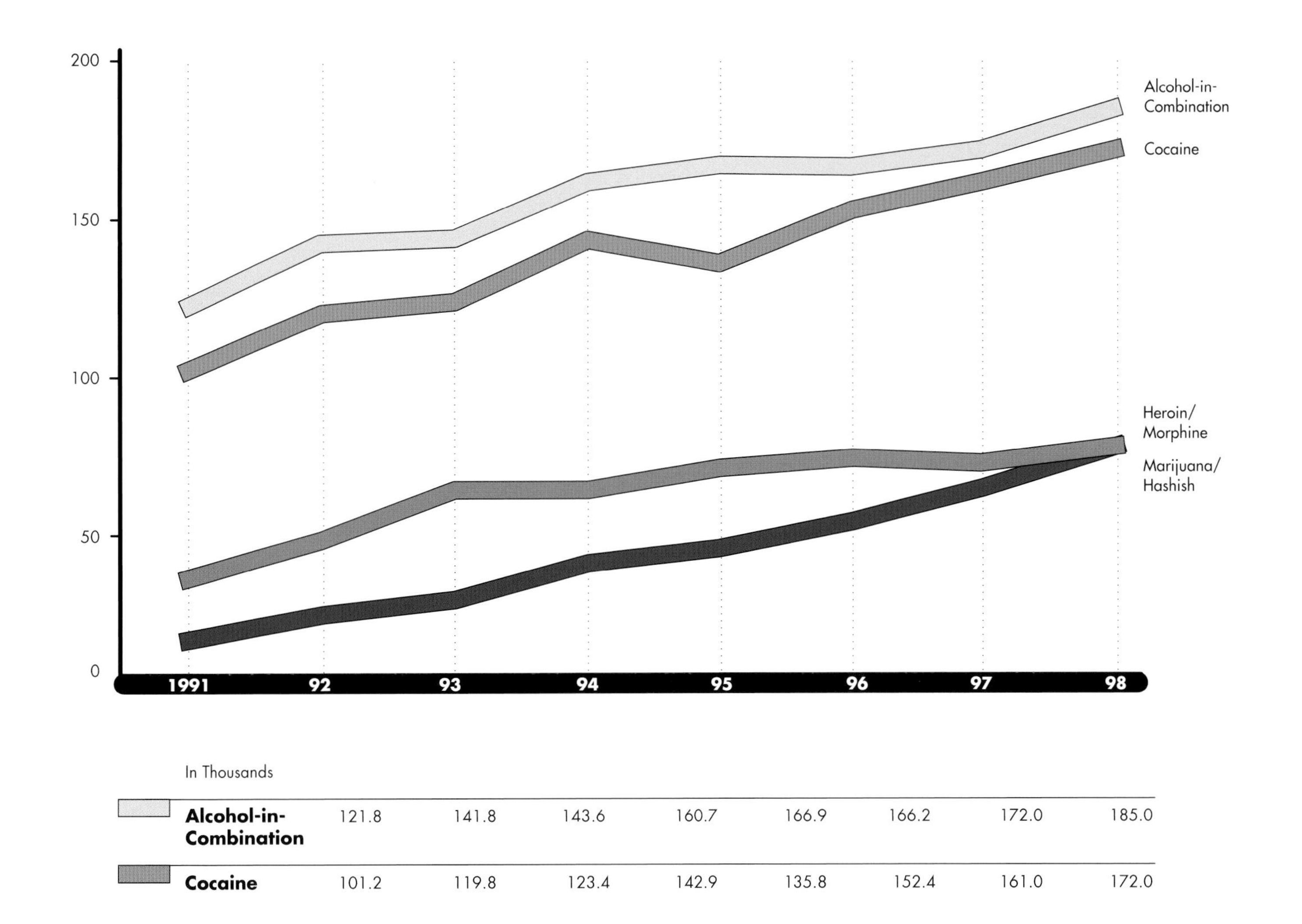

In Thousands

	1991	92	93	94	95	96	97	98
Alcohol-in-Combination	121.8	141.8	143.6	160.7	166.9	166.2	172.0	185.0
Cocaine	101.2	119.8	123.4	142.9	135.8	152.4	161.0	172.0
Heroin/ Morphine	35.9	48.0	63.2	64.0	70.8	74.0	72.0	77.6
Marijuana/ Hashish	16.3	24.0	28.9	40.2	45.3	53.8	64.7	76.9

NOTES: Estimates of selected drug mentions are for the lower 48 states. A drug mention refers to a substance (as many as four) mentioned during a single drug-related episode. A drug episode is an emergency department visit that was related to the use of an illegal drug(s) or the nonmedical use of a legal drug for patients age 6 and older. Alcohol is reported in this survey only when used in combination with another drug (alcohol-in-combination).

SOURCE: U.S. Substance Abuse and Mental Health Services Administration, Office of Applied Studies. *Year-End 1998 Emergency Department Data from the Drug Abuse Warning Network.* Rockville, MD, 1999.

holics and drug abusers. Care in these specialty centers accounts for less than one-third of total alcohol (22 percent) and drug (31 percent) direct health care costs; alcohol prevention and support services account for 8 percent, and drug abuse prevention and support services for 13 percent.

Also significant are the costs of treatment for specific health problems attributed to alcohol and drug abuse. For example, 10 percent of alcohol health care costs are for care of fetal alcohol syndrome, and 37 percent of drug abuse health care costs are HIV/AIDS-related.

Alcohol, tobacco and illicit drug abuse account for a significant portion of health care spending covered by public funders. Almost 20 percent of all Medicaid hospital costs, and nearly $1 of every $4 Medicare spends on inpatient hospital care, is associated with substance abuse. An even higher proportion (29 percent) of the costs of Veterans' Health Services may be attributable to substance abuse, in part because the Department of Veterans' Affairs offers more extensive substance abuse treatment services. Even more striking, federal and state sources pay for more than 43 percent of total smoking-attributable health care expenditures. On average, more than 14 percent of Medicaid expenditures in all states in 1993 were attributable to cigarette smoking.

Indicator 22

Health Care Costs of Substance Abuse Top $114 Billion, 1995

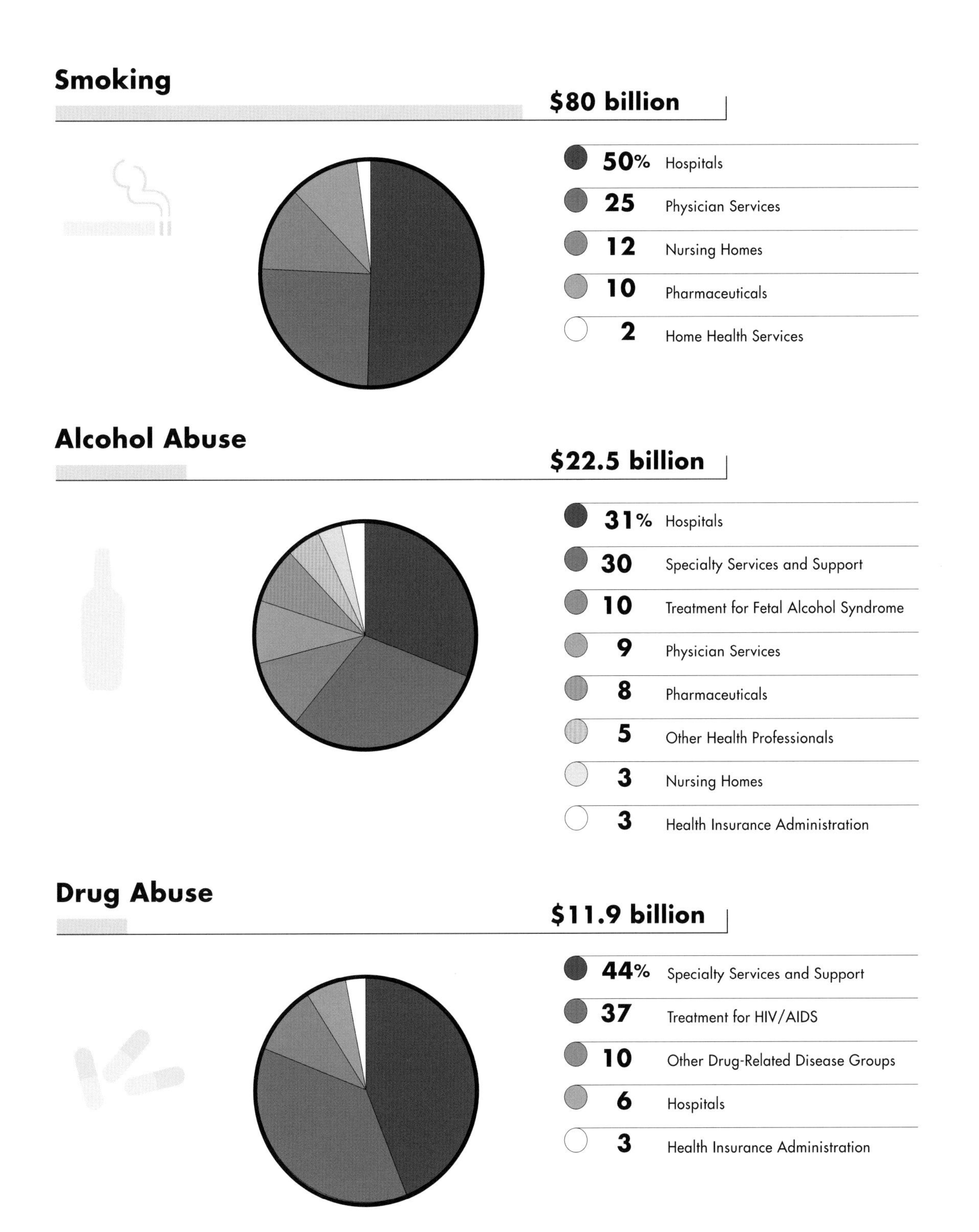

NOTES: Percentages may not add up to 100 due to rounding.

SOURCES: Smoking: Unpublished data for 1995 from Rice DP. Institute for Health and Aging, University of California at San Francisco, CA. Alcohol and drug abuse: Unpublished data for 1995 from Henrick Harwood, The Lewin Group, Inc., Falls Church, VA.

Effects of Substance Abuse on Families

Substance abuse places tremendous psychological and financial burdens on families, and many people report alcoholism or drug abuse among their relatives. Among adult current drinkers, 56 percent say they have a blood relative who is or was an alcoholic or problem drinker (Indicator 23). Moreover, 25 percent report that one or more parent was an alcoholic or problem drinker. Three out of 10 adults report that drinking has been a cause of trouble in their family, and nearly 20 percent say that drug abuse has been a source of family problems. As high as these figures are, the prevalence of substance abuse and family problems is believed to be seriously underreported.

Alcohol abuse can affect a family in many ways, even causing its breakup. Among adult current drinkers, separated and divorced adults are three times as likely as their married counterparts to have been married to or lived with an alcoholic or problem drinker. In addition, more than 40 percent of separated or divorced women were married to or lived with a problem drinker or alcoholic, compared with less than 20 percent of separated or divorced men. Problem drinking may be defined as alcohol consumption—chronic or acute—that results in social, legal, medical or other problems.

One of the most troubling effects of alcohol on marriage is the relationship between heavy drinking and marital violence. Illicit drugs as well as alcohol may also play a role in domestic violence, which affects both married and unmarried couples. More than three-quarters of female victims of nonfatal domestic violence reported that their assailant had been drinking or using drugs (Indicator 24).

Families with substance-abusing parents experience a host of other social problems, such as a higher risk of raising children who use alcohol and drugs themselves. Children from these families are also more likely to have problems with delinquency, poor school performance and emotional difficulties, such as aggressive behavior and bouts of hyperactivity, than their peers whose parents do not abuse alcohol or drugs. The number of children at risk because of parental substance abuse is substantial: In 1996, three million children under age 18 lived with a parent who was dependent on illicit drugs, and six million lived with a parent who was dependent on alcohol.

Reports of child neglect and abuse have increased dramatically in recent years, and many such incidents are believed to be directly related to illicit drug—and possibly

Indicator 23

More than Half of Current Drinkers Have a Family History of Alcoholism

Percent of Current Drinkers with a Relative Who Has Been an Alcoholic or Problem Drinker

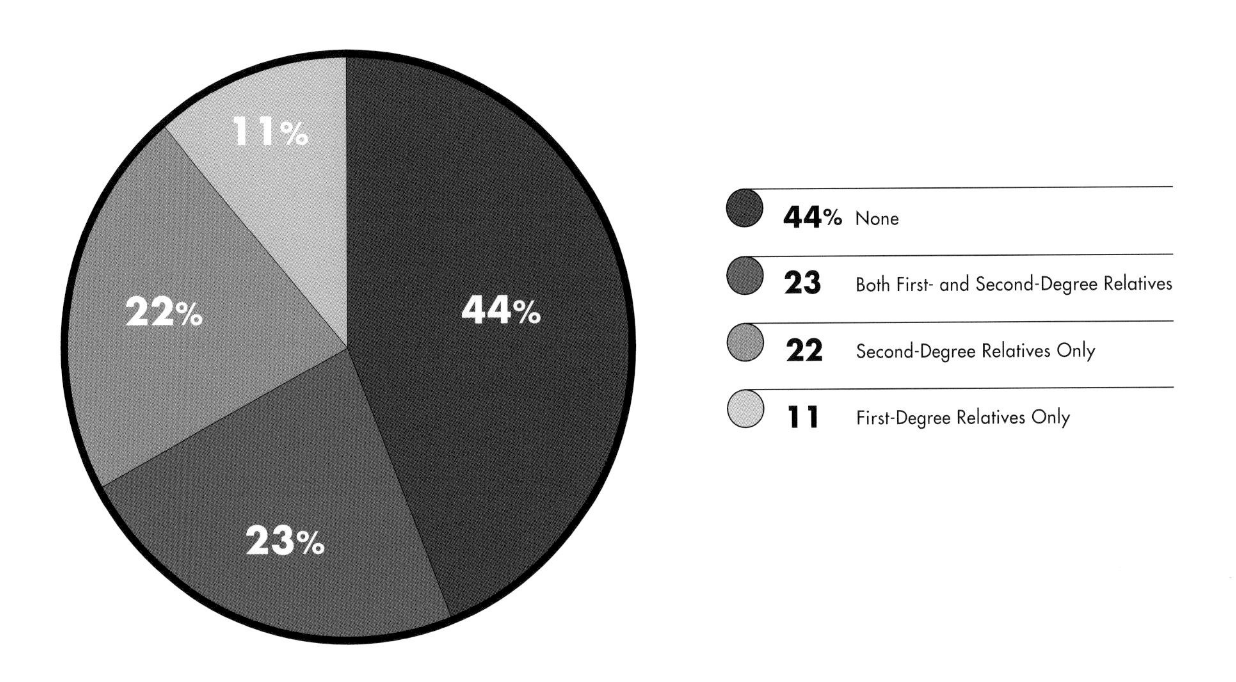

NOTES: In this study, current drinkers are defined as those who had 12 or more drinks of alcohol in the past year. An alcoholic or problem drinker is defined as a person who has physical or emotional problems because of drinking; problems with a spouse, family or friends because of drinking; problems at work because of drinking; problems with the police because of drinking, such as drunk driving; or a person who seems to spend a lot of time drinking or being hungover. The type of relative who has been an alcoholic or problem drinker can be either a blood or nonblood relative. Blood relatives can be further classified as first-degree or second-degree relatives. First-degree relatives are biological parents or children and full siblings. Second-degree relatives are natural parents' biological parents, full siblings of either natural parent and half siblings of the respondent on either natural parent's side.

SOURCE: Stinson FS, Yi H, Grant BF, Chou P, Dawson DA, Pickering R. "Drinking in the United States: Main Findings from the 1992 National Longitudinal Alcohol Epidemiologic Survey (NLAES)." *U.S. Alcohol Epidemiologic Data Reference Manual, Vol. 6.* Bethesda, MD: National Institute on Alcohol Abuse and Alcoholism, 1998.

Effects of Substance Abuse on Families (continued)

alcohol use—among parents. Alcohol and drug abuse are factors in the placement of more than three-quarters of children entering foster care.

Children whose parents smoke have more health problems, such as ear infections, asthma, respiratory infections and decreased pulmonary function. They miss one-third more school days and have 21 percent more days of restricted activities, such as missing after-school sports practice, than unexposed children.

Another impact of substance abuse on families is the financial drain. The costs of drinking and smoking can be high. These costs are calculated for all households, not just those with drinkers and smokers; for example, almost $900 a year can be spent on four six-packs of beer a week, and a two-pack-a-day smoker can spend several thousand dollars a year on cigarettes, but this can vary widely due to differences in state taxes. If the impact of cocaine use and other illicit drugs were calculated, the effects on a family budget would be staggering.

Indicator 24

Alcohol Use Is Prevalent among Domestic Abusers

Percent of Female Victims of Nonfatal Intimate Violence Reporting Alcohol or Drug Use by Assailant

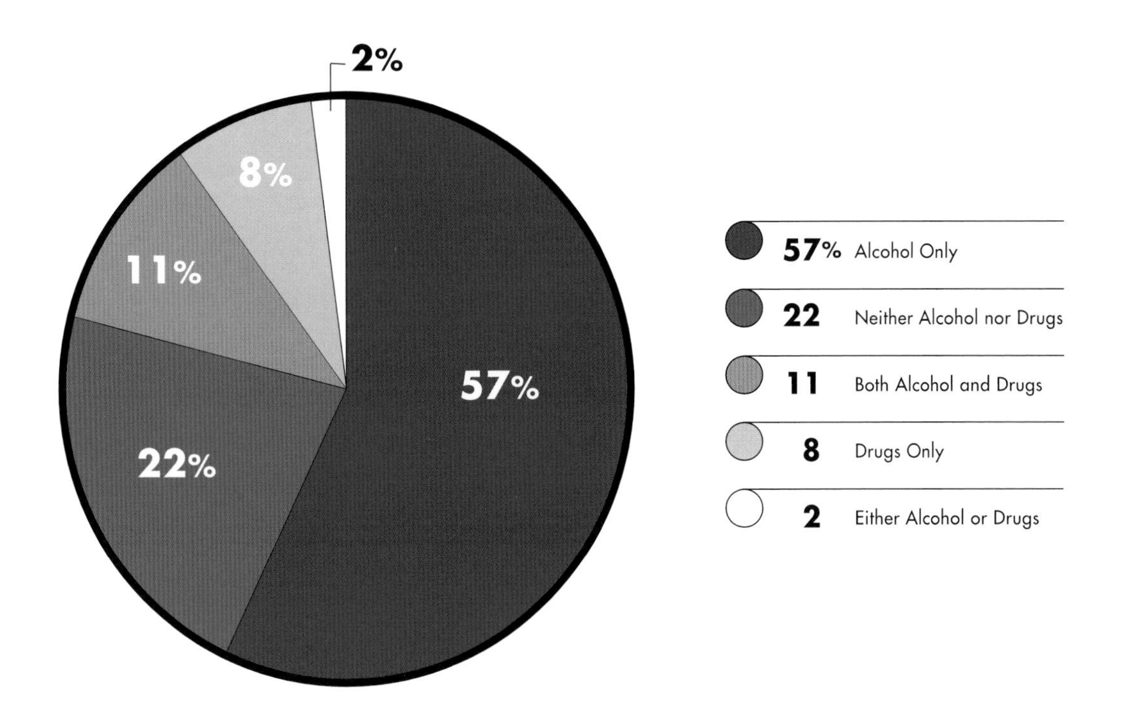

NOTES: Assailant includes current or former spouse, boyfriend or girlfriend. Domestic violence between intimates in this survey includes nonfatal violence: rapes, robberies or assaults. Because these data are based on victim's perceptions of violence, murders and manslaughter are not included, although they are part of domestic violence. These data include both incidents reported and those not reported to the police and exclude victims who were not able to distinguish alcohol or drug use by the offender.

SOURCE: Data are from the National Crime Victimization Survey, as reported in: U.S. Department of Justice, Bureau of Justice Statistics. *Alcohol and Crime, 1998.*

Relationship to Crime

Consequences of Use

The link between alcohol or illicit drug use and crime is visible every day in courtrooms, jails and prisons across the country. Many arrestees were under the influence of alcohol, illicit drugs or both when they committed their crime. Others sold drugs illegally. In 1997, more than 2.5 million arrests were made for alcohol offenses (driving under the influence, liquor law violations, drunkenness, disorderly conduct and vagrancy) and more than 1.5 million for drug offenses. Drug offenses include drug trafficking, possession and other drug offenses, such as manufacturing.

Alcohol and illicit drugs are involved in many violent crimes and other serious offenses. For example, at least half of the adults arrested for major crimes, such as homicide, theft and assault, and more than eight in ten arrested for drug offenses, tested positive for drugs at the time of their arrest (Indicator 25). Similarly, among juvenile arrestees, use of illicit drugs around the time of the arrest is high, although they are less likely to test positive for recent drug use than are adults. About half of state prison inmates and 40 percent of federal prisoners incarcerated for committing violent crimes report that they were under the influence of alcohol or drugs at the time of their offense.

Overall, about three-quarters of all prisoners in 1997 were involved with alcohol or drug abuse in some way in the time leading up to their current offense—including those who used drugs in the month before the offense, those under the influence of alcohol or drugs at the time of their offense and those who had been convicted of a drug offense. Among federal prisoners, conviction for a drug offense accounted for the bulk (63 percent) of involvement; nearly 45 percent of federal prisoners abused drugs in the month before the offense, and 34 percent were using alcohol or drugs at the time of their offense. Among state prisoners, those who used drugs in the month before the offense (57 percent) and those under the influence of alcohol or drugs at the time of the offense (52 percent) accounted for the largest share of prisoners involved with alcohol or drug abuse, while 21 percent of state prisoners had a current drug offense.

Alcohol is more likely to be involved in crimes against people than property. In about one-half to two-thirds of homicides and serious assaults, alcohol is present in the offender, the victim or both. Alcohol is often involved in rape and other sexual assaults. According to one estimate, up to 60 percent of sexual offenders were drinking at the time of the offense.

Indicator 25

Many Arrestees Test Positive for Drugs, 1995

Percent of Arrestees Testing Positive by Charge at Arrest

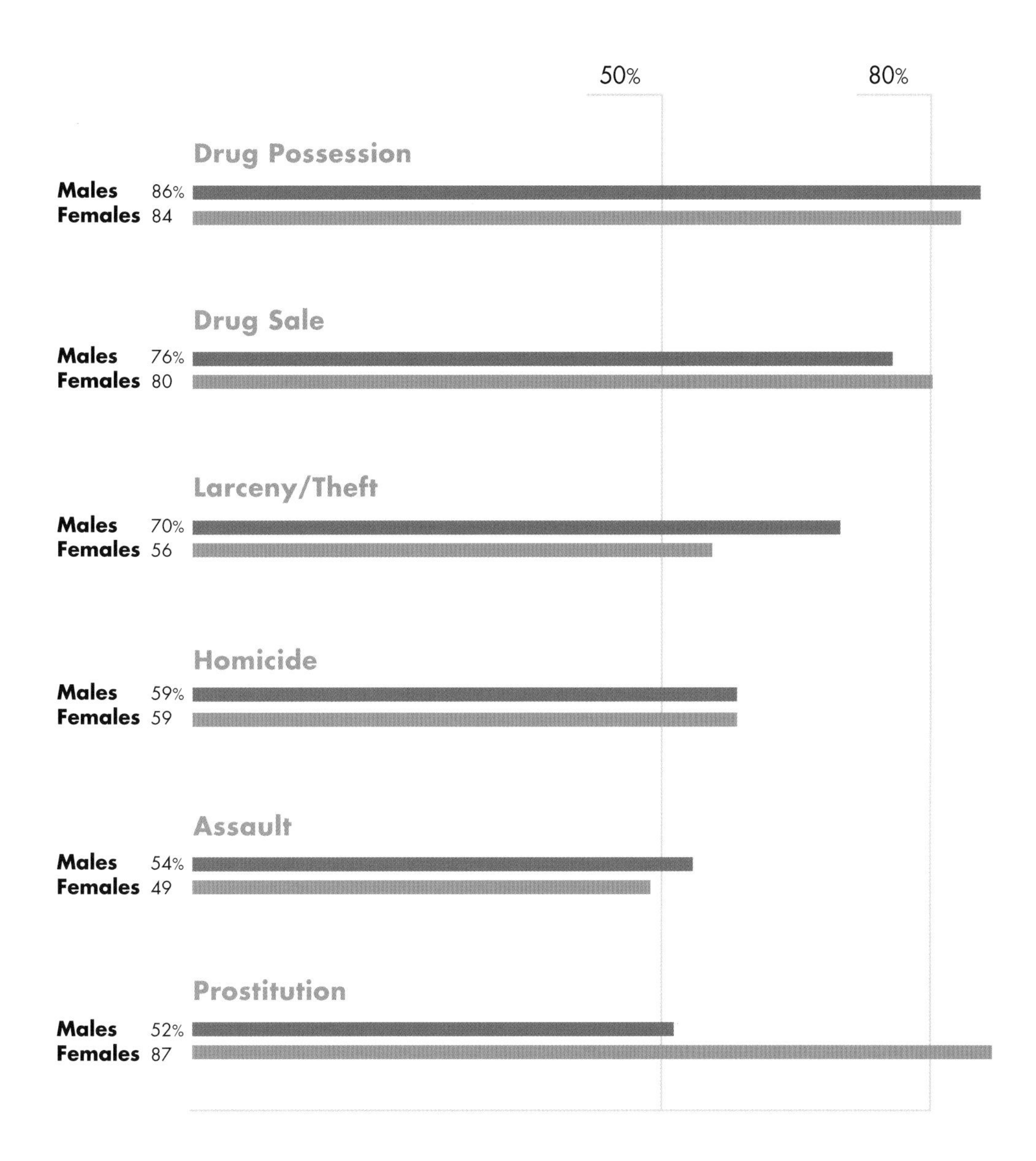

NOTES: Testing using urinalysis is done for cocaine, opiates, marijuana, PCP, methadone, benzodiazepines, methaqualone, propoxyphene, barbiturates and amphetamines. Data were collected in 23 cities. Female arrestees were not tested in two cities.

SOURCES: White House Office of National Drug Control Policy. *Fact Sheet: Drug-Related Crime.* Rockville, MD: Drug Policy Information Clearinghouse, 1997. Table 2, p. 2. Table 2 data from a special data analysis of the U.S. Department of Justice, National Institute of Justice. *1995 Drug Use Forecasting Report on Adult and Juvenile Arrestees*, 1996.

Although women make up only a small proportion of inmates (7.4 percent in federal prisons, 6.3 percent in state prisons and 10.8 percent in local jails), illicit drugs often play a role in their crimes. Among state prison inmates in 1997, for example, females were more likely than males to have used illicit drugs in the month prior to the offense (62 percent vs. 56 percent), and to have been under their influence at the time of the offense (40 percent vs. 32 percent). However, male federal prisoners reported higher past month drug use than female federal prisoners (45 percent vs. 37 percent). Alcohol abuse may be more prevalent among male prisoners. Among state and federal prison inmates, males were more likely than females to have been drinking at the time of offense (38 and 21 percent, respectively, vs. 29 and 15 percent, respectively).

Drug offenders increasingly fill the nation's prisons (Indicator 26). In 1997, 70 percent of drug offenders in state prisons and 86 percent of drug offenders in federal prisons were serving time for drug trafficking or possession with intent to distribute. From 1985 to 1995, the proportion of drug offenders in state prisons increased from 9 percent to 23 percent of all state prisoners, and the proportion of federal inmates sentenced for drug offenses grew from 34 percent to 60 percent. Drug offenders have accounted for more than one-third of the growth in the state prison population and more than 80 percent of the increase in the number of federal prison inmates since 1985. In addition, more than one in three women in state prisons was serving a sentence for drug offenses in 1997, up from one in eight in 1986. These increases in incarcerated drug offenders are related, in part, to mandatory minimum sentencing laws for drug offenses, and are often cited as major reasons for prison overcrowding.

Indicator 26

Number of Drug Offenders in Prison Soars

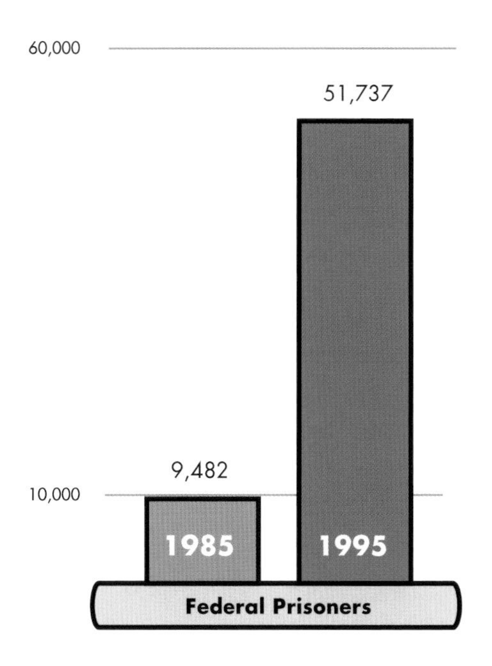

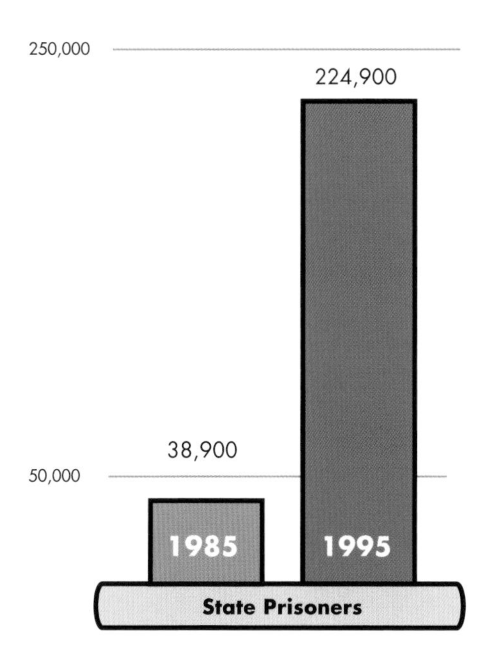

SOURCE: U.S. Department of Justice, Bureau of Justice Statistics. *Prisoners in 1996*. Washington, DC: Bureau of Justice Statistics, 1997. Table 13, p. 10; Table 14, p. 11.

Workplace Burden

Section 2

Consequences of Use

A significant amount of substance use takes place among the American work force, and some of this use occurs on the job or just prior to going to work. One-third of full-time workers are smokers, more than one-fifth reported binge drinking in the past month and approximately 12 percent say they used illicit drugs during the past year. Workers are three times more likely to report dependence on alcohol than on illicit drugs. Substance abuse can create hazards, not only for employees, but also for co-workers and the public. Substance abuse among transportation workers, for example, can endanger the lives of passengers and bystanders.

Smoking is a costly burden for employers. In addition to health care costs for the smokers, smoking poses health hazards to nonsmokers at work. In one recent study, more than one-third of workers reported being bothered regularly by workplace smoke. Protection from environmental tobacco smoke in the workplace varies by occupation and age, with food service workers and teenagers the least likely of all employees in the United States to work in a smoke-free environment. Fifty-four percent of white-collar employees are covered by a smoke-free policy, compared with only 35 percent of service workers and 27 percent of blue-collar workers.

Alcohol and illicit drug use are also costly to employers. Health care costs for employees with alcohol problems are about twice those of other employees. Added to this are the costs of related workplace injuries—including those in company-owned vehicles, higher employee turnover and lost productivity. One recent study of 14,000 employees at seven Fortune 500 companies found that employees who are not alcohol dependent but who occasionally drink too much cause most alcohol-related work performance problems, not alcohol-dependent drinkers, as commonly believed. Although the rate of alcohol-related work problems is lower among nondependent drinkers than among alcohol-dependent workers, the number of nondependent drinkers at the workplace vastly outweighs the number of dependent drinkers on the job, and thus their alcohol-related work productivity problems in total exceed those of dependent workers.

Substance abuse is also more common in certain occupations and industries. Heavy alcohol and illicit drug use is highest among construction workers and food preparers. Auto mechanics, laborers and light-truck drivers are among those more susceptible to alcohol abuse. And tobacco use is more common among blue-collar workers than white-collar workers.

Indicator 27

Nearly Three-Fourths of Illicit Drug Users Are Employed, 1997

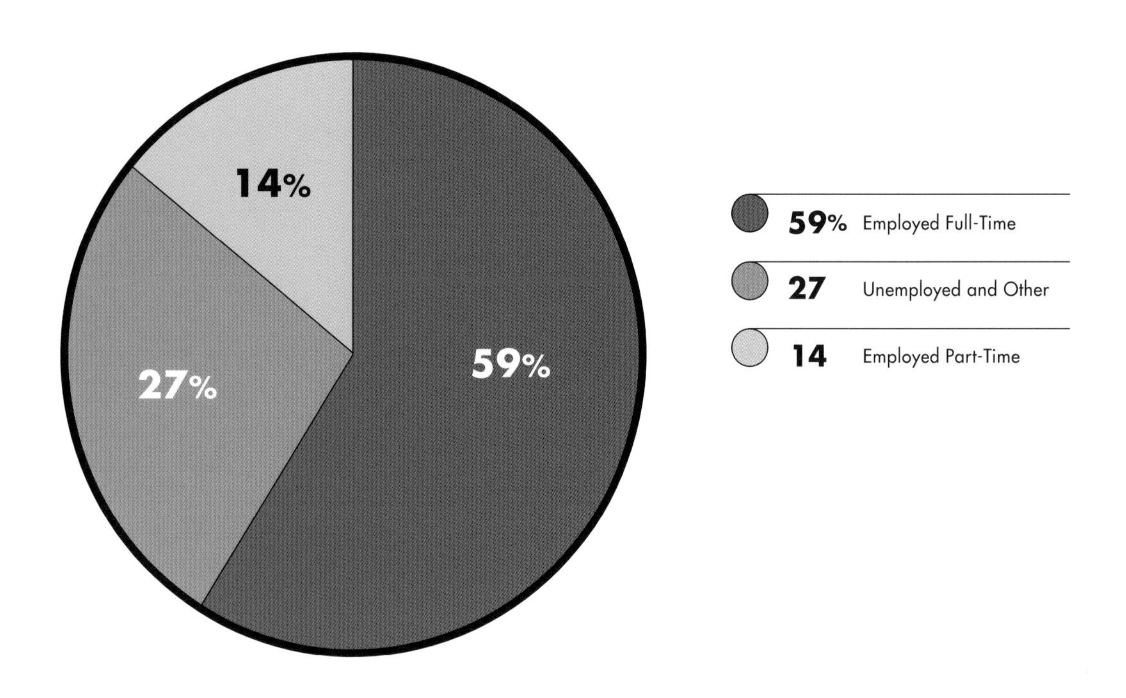

NOTES: Other includes people who are retired, disabled, homemakers and students. Illicit drug users include all current illicit drug users age 18 and older.

SOURCE: Data are preliminary results from the 1997 National Household Survey on Drug Abuse, as reported at: www.health.org/pubs/97hhs/nhsda978.htm

Almost three-quarters of illicit drug users work full- or part-time (Indicator 27), but their work record is problematic. Heavy drinkers and illicit drug users were more likely than those who did not drink heavily or use drugs to have skipped work in the past month or to have worked for three or more employers in the past year. Eleven percent of heavy alcohol users and 13 percent of illicit drug users had skipped work in the past month (Indicator 28). According to a recent poll, more than 60 percent of respondents said they know people who went to work under the influence of alcohol or drugs, but less than 20 percent of those surveyed ever approached a co-worker about his or her substance use.

Since evidence shows that treatment can reduce job-related problems and result in abstinence, many employers sponsor employee assistance programs (EAPs), conduct drug testing or have policies or procedures to detect use of illicit drugs or alcohol and promote early treatment. In a recent national study, half of all full-time employees age 18 to 49 reported access to an EAP or other types of counseling programs for substance abuse-related problems. Having access to an EAP, however, varied by establishment size, and was highest for employees in large establishments (83 percent), followed by workers in mid-size establishments (59 percent) and small establishments (24 percent). Similarly, although 44 percent of employees said they work in establishments with a drug testing program, people employed in smaller establishments were less likely than those working for larger companies to report that their workplace tests employees for alcohol or drug use. Drug testing is also higher for people in protective services and transportation occupations than for those in other jobs, perhaps due to the special safety concerns of these types of work or federal regulations that mandate drug testing for certain employees.

Indicator 28

Alcohol and Drug Users Have Problems Working, 1997

Full-Time Employees, Ages 18–49

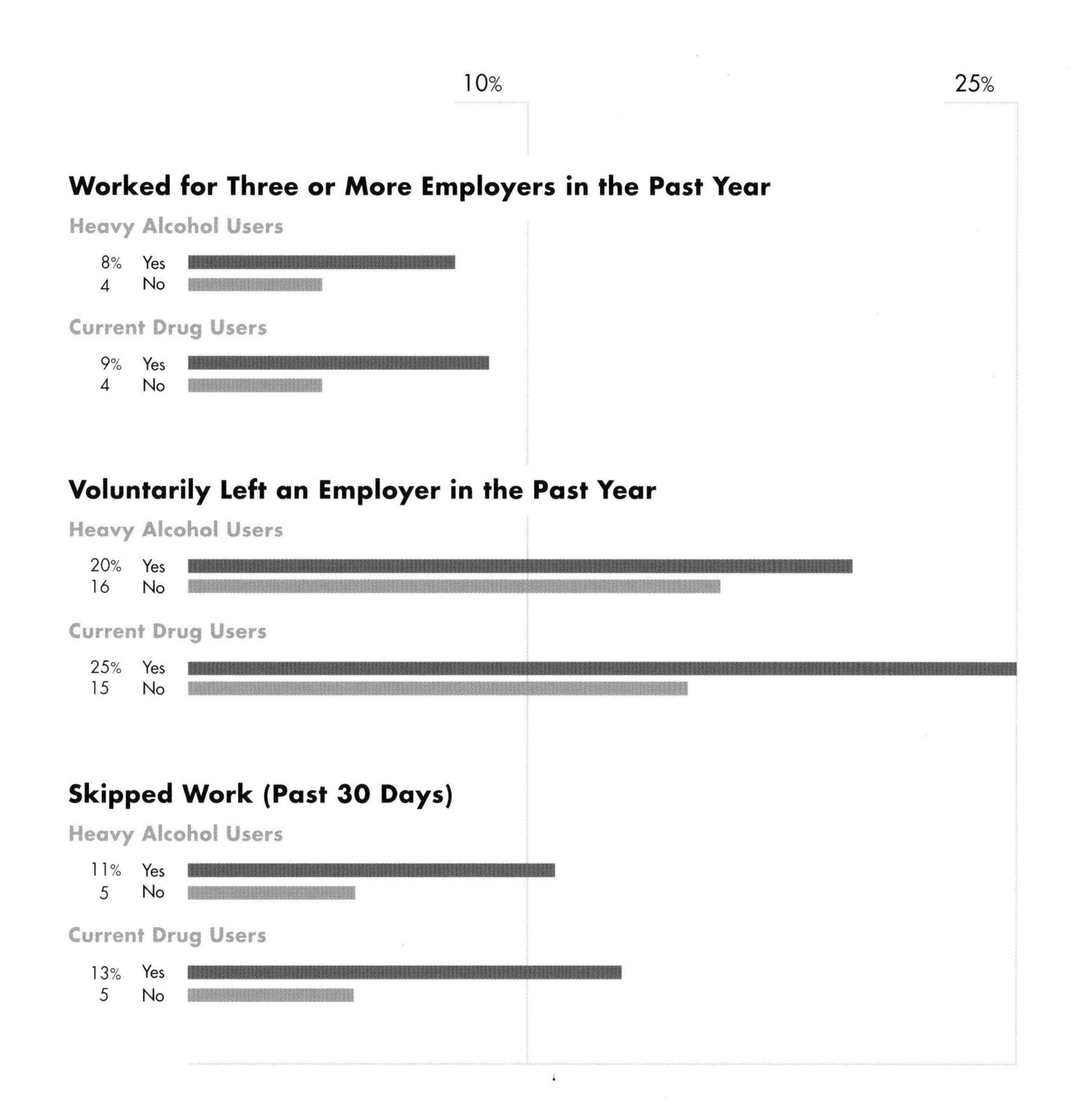

NOTES: Heavy alcohol users are people who drank five or more drinks per occasion on five or more days in the past 30 days. Current drug users are people who used any illicit drug in the past month. Skipped work refers to one or more unexcused absences from work in the past month. No refers to those who are either not current drug users or are not current heavy alcohol users.

SOURCE: Zhang Z, Huang LX, Brittingham AM. *Worker Drug Use and Workplace Policies and Programs: Results from the 1994 and 1997 NHSDA.* Rockville, MD: U.S. Substance Abuse and Mental Health Services Administration, Office of Applied Studies, 1999.

Consequences of Use

GENERAL

Institute of Medicine. *Pathways of Addiction: Opportunities in Drug Abuse Research.* Washington, DC: National Academy Press, 1996.

National Center for Health Statistics. *Health United States 1998 with Socioeconomic Status and Health Chartbook.* Hyattsville, MD, 1998.

National Institute on Alcohol Abuse and Alcoholism. *Tenth Special Report to the U.S. Congress on Alcohol and Health from the Secretary of Health and Human Services.* Rockville, MD, 2000.

TOBACCO DEATHS

California Environmental Protection Agency, Office of Environmental Health Hazard Assessment. *Health Effects of Exposure to Environmental Tobacco Smoke: Final Report.* Sacramento, CA, 1997.

U.S. Centers for Disease Control and Prevention. "Projected Smoking-Related Deaths Among Youth—United States." *Morbidity and Mortality Weekly Report,* 45(44): 971–974, 1996.

U.S. Centers for Disease Control and Prevention. "Smoking-Attributable Mortality and Years of Potential Life Lost—United States, 1984." Editorial Note—1997. *Morbidity and Mortality Weekly Report,* 46(20): 444–451, 1997.

ALCOHOL DEATHS

Hingson R and Howland J. "Alcohol and Non-Traffic Unintended Injuries." *Addiction,* 88(7): 877–883, 1993.

Stinson FS and Nephew TM. "State Trends in Alcohol-Related Mortality, 1979–92." *U.S. Alcohol Epidemiologic Data Reference Manual, Vol. 5.* Bethesda, MD: National Institute on Alcohol Abuse and Alcoholism, 1996.

U.S. Centers for Disease Control and Prevention. "Involvement by Young Drivers in Fatal Motor-Vehicle Crashes—United States, 1988–1995." *Morbidity and Mortality Weekly Report,* 45(48): 1049–1053, 1996.

ILLICIT DRUG DEATHS

Anderson RN, Kochanek KD and Murphy SL. "Report of Final Mortality Statistics, 1995." *Monthly Vital Statistics Report,* 45(11), Supp. 2. Hyattsville, MD: National Center for Health Statistics, 1997.

U.S. Centers for Disease Control and Prevention. "Update: Trends in AIDS Incidence, Deaths, and Prevalence—United States, 1996." *Morbidity and Mortality Weekly Report,* 46(8): 165–173, 1997.

U.S. Substance Abuse and Mental Health Services Administration, Office of Applied Studies. *Drug Abuse Warning Network Annual Medical Examiner Data 1995.* Rockville, MD, 1997.

STRAINS ON THE NATION'S HEALTH CARE SYSTEM

Fox K, Merrill JC, Chang H and Califano JA. "Estimating the Costs of Substance Abuse to the Medicaid Hospital Care Program." *American Journal of Public Health,* 85(1): 48–54, 1995.

Harwood H, Fountain D and Livermore G. *The Economic Costs of Alcohol and Drug Abuse in the United States, 1992.* Fairfax, VA: National Institute on Drug Abuse and the National Institute on Alcohol Abuse and Alcoholism, 1998.

Stoddard JJ and Gray B. "Maternal Smoking and Medical Expenditures for Childhood Respiratory Illness." *American Journal of Public Health,* 87(2): 205–209, 1997.

U.S. Centers for Disease Control and Prevention. "Medical-Care Expenditures Attributable to Cigarette Smoking—United States, 1993." *Morbidity and Mortality Weekly Report,* 43(26): 469–472, 1994.

EFFECTS OF SUBSTANCE ABUSE ON FAMILIES

Kelleher K, Chaffin M, Hollenberg J and Fischer E. "Alcohol and Drug Disorders Among Physically Abusive and Neglectful Parents in a Community-Based Sample." *American Journal of Public Health,* 84(10): 1586–1590, 1994.

Leonard KE and Roberts LJ. "Alcohol in the Early Years of Marriage." *Alcohol Health and Research World,* 20(3): 192–196, 1996.

Mayes LC. "Substance Abuse and Parenting." In Bornstein MH (ed.). *The Handbook of Parenting.* Mahwah, NJ: Erlbaum, 1995, pp. 101–125.

Windle M. "Effect of Parental Drinking on Adolescents." *Alcohol Health and Research World,* 20(3): 181–184, 1996.

RELATIONSHIP TO CRIME

Collins JJ and Messerschmidt PM. "Epidemiology of Alcohol-Related Violence." *Alcohol Health and Research World,* 17(2): 93–100, 1993.

U.S. Department of Justice, Bureau of Justice Statistics. *Drugs, Crime, and the Justice System: A National Report from the Bureau of Justice Statistics.* Washington, DC, 1992.

U.S. Department of Justice, Bureau of Justice Statistics. *Sourcebook of Criminal Justice Statistics, 1998.* Washington, DC, 1999.

WORKPLACE BURDEN

Gerlach KK, Shopland DR, Hartman AM, Gibson JT and Pechacek TF. "Workplace Smoking Policies in the United States: Results from a National Survey of More than 100,000 Workers." *Tobacco Control,* 6: 199–206, 1997.

Hoffman JP, Brittingham A and Larison C. *Drug Use Among U.S. Workers: Prevalence and Trends by Occupation and Industry Categories.* Rockville, MD: U.S. Substance Abuse and Mental Health Services Administration, Office of Applied Studies, 1996.

Zhang Z, Huang LX and Brittingham AM. *Worker Drug Use and Workplace Policies and Programs: Results from the 1994 and 1997 NHSDA.* Rockville, MD: U.S. Substance Abuse and Mental Health Services Administration, Office of Applied Studies, 1999.

Combating the Problem

- Polls show that more than half of Americans strongly believe that drug treatment should be more available.
- In 1998, the tobacco industry spent more than $6 billion on advertising and product promotion.
- Even though two-thirds of the federal drug control budget goes for law enforcement and interdiction, the flow of illicit drugs into the United States remains high.
- Public awareness campaigns are used by community-based groups as a way to increase knowledge about and change community attitudes toward substance abuse.
- At 30 percent of the retail price, on average, the U.S. cigarette tax is one of the lowest in the developed world. Increasing tobacco taxes would cut tobacco use.
- All states now have legal intoxication levels of 0.02 or less for drivers under age 21—far below the 0.08 or 0.10 levels required for people 21 and older.
- Although it is illegal to sell and distribute tobacco products to youth under age 18, most underage smokers are able to buy tobacco products.
- More than 18 million alcohol abusers and 5 million illicit drug abusers need treatment, but only a small number receive it.
- The improvement rate for people completing substance abuse treatment is comparable to that of people treated for asthma and other chronic, relapsing health conditions.
- Most of the 47 million American adults who currently smoke would like to quit, but few smokers are counseled by their doctors about quitting.

Public Attitudes

Section 3

Combating the Problem

According to current opinion surveys, illicit drug abuse is one of the most important problems facing the United States. More than 50 percent of those surveyed in a 1999 Gallup poll said that their concern about illicit drug use had grown in the past five years, and use among adolescents in particular is a top concern of Americans. More than half of the respondents to a 1997 national survey cited illicit drugs as the most important problem facing American children today. This may be related in part to a rising awareness of the consequences of substance abuse and to greater health consciousness. Another factor may be the association between illicit drugs and the nation's concerns about crime.

Public opinion about the importance of drugs as a national problem runs a cyclical course. In the late 1980s, it was the number one problem most often cited by respondents in opinion polls, but in the early '80s and early '90s, it was cited much less frequently. Such variation raises the question of whether public opinion accurately reflects the severity of the problem or is instead determined by multiple causes, including greater media coverage.

Researchers are finding that many factors are associated with public attitudes about national problems, such as the local context in which the people who were polled live. It is not surprising that the drug problem is more important to those living in neighborhoods where the sale and use of illicit drugs is highly visible. In a 1995 survey of inner-city communities with high poverty, unemployment, crime and other harms associated with drug use, drugs were rated as the second most important problem facing the nation—behind crime.

Most Americans say they believe that the risks from excessive alcohol, tobacco and illicit drug use are high (Indicator 29), and they endorse restrictions associated with their use. The vast majority of Americans consider underage drinking to be a major concern, and many adults favor stronger regulations to reduce teenagers' access to alcohol. For example, 83 percent of adults surveyed said that adults who illegally give alcohol to minors should be penalized. A 1996 Gallup poll reported that 71 percent of respondents favored a law requiring teenagers to pass a drug test before they could get a driver's license, and 68 percent favored drug testing for anyone seeking a driver's license. About

Indicator 29

Attitudes about Risk and Substance Use Vary by Age, 1998

Percent Who See Great Risk in Using Substances by Age Group

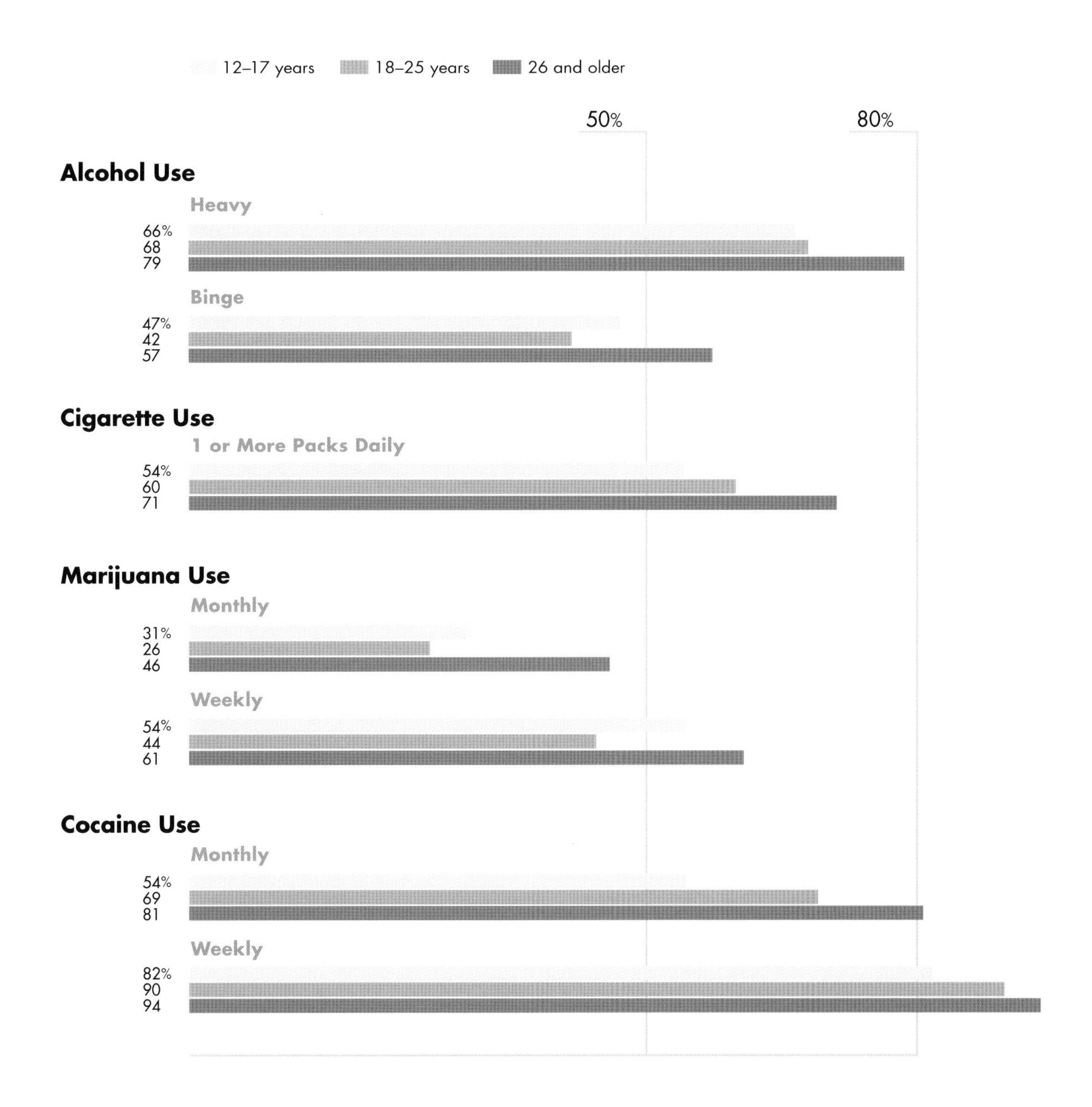

NOTES: Heavy alcohol use is having four or five drinks nearly every day. Binge drinking is having five or more drinks once or twice a week.

SOURCE: U.S. Substance Abuse and Mental Health Services Administration, Office of Applied Studies. *Summary of Findings from the 1998 National Household Survey on Drug Abuse.* Rockville, MD, 1999. Table 57.

32 percent of people polled also thought a driver's license should be revoked for those convicted more than once of drunk driving.

Americans also view smoking as a serious problem, especially for teenagers, but they rank smoking much lower than other problems facing teenagers in 1999, including illicit drugs and alcohol. While not a top priority for the public, new legislation is favored by Americans to lower teenage smoking, as are more education programs to discourage underage smoking.

In 1999, about two-thirds of Americans opposed legalizing marijuana. This reflects a more liberal view of this issue than in 1990, when 81 percent of people were against legalization (Indicator 30). Although two-thirds oppose legalizing marijuana, almost three-quarters think it should be made legally available to physicians to prescribe to patients to reduce pain and suffering.

Attitudes about how to deal with illicit drug abuse are mixed. Although more than 75 percent of Americans believe that the War on Drugs has failed, they continue to want greater resources spent on these efforts, such as more money to stop the flow of drugs into the United States or increased funding for police. At the same time, the public increasingly supports anti-drug education, and in 1996 almost half thought more money should be spent educating youth and adults about the dangers of drugs. In 1999, 81 percent of respondents polled said it was extremely important for the U.S. government to spend tax dollars on lowering illicit drug use among America's youth. More than 80 percent of Americans polled agreed that more drug treatment should be made available, and about half of those polled also agreed that treatment and rehabilitation programs usually work.

Indicator 30

Most Americans Still against Legalization of Marijuana, though Opposition Has Declined

Percent Who Believe Marijuana Should Not Be Legalized

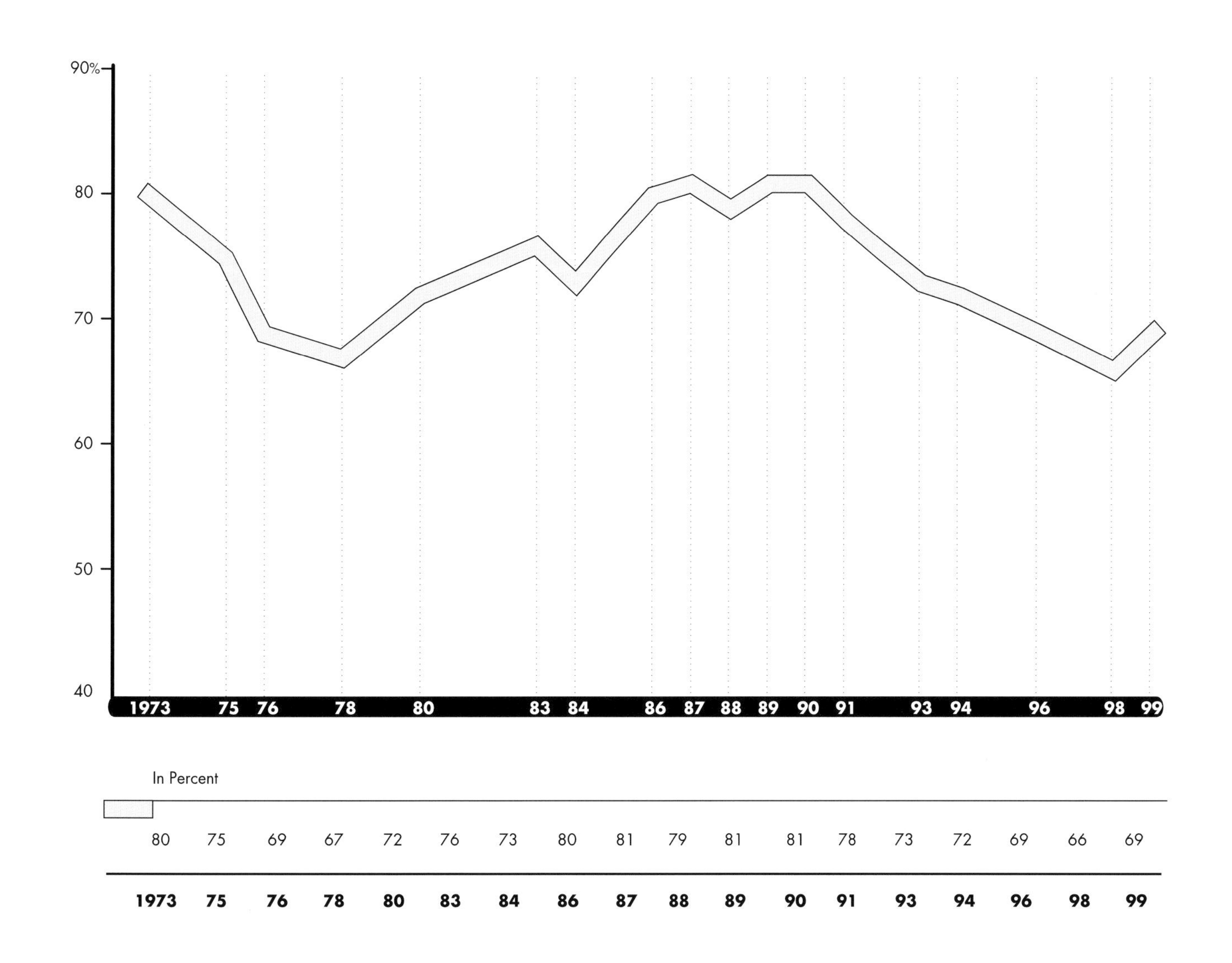

1973	75	76	78	80	83	84	86	87	88	89	90	91	93	94	96	98	99
80	75	69	67	72	76	73	80	81	79	81	81	78	73	72	69	66	69

SOURCES: For 1973–1998: National Opinion Research Center. *General Social Surveys, 1972–98.* Storrs, CT: The Roper Center for Public Opinion Research, University of Connecticut. For 1999: *The Gallup Poll Monthly*, no. 402. Data reported in the *Sourcebook of Criminal Justice Statistics, Online.* www.albany.edu/Sourcebook

The Media

Section 3

Combating the Problem

Social scientists have long considered the mass media to be a powerful influence on individual beliefs, values and behaviors. Recent research suggests that repeated exposure to positive media portrayals or product advertising fosters positive feelings toward the use of alcohol, tobacco and illicit drugs.

The tobacco industry spent more than $6 billion for advertising and product promotion in 1998 (Indicator 31). Promotion as a proportion of total cigarette advertising and and promotional expenditures has increased dramatically in the 1990s. Although banned from direct advertising on television in 1971, tobacco products are highly visible to viewers. For example, in 1999, 44 percent of non-news programs aired by the four major television networks portrayed tobacco use in at least one episode.

Perhaps because of its inability to advertise on television, the tobacco industry is the second largest advertiser in the print media, including magazines and newspapers, and was, until recently, the largest advertiser on billboards. While the only restriction on tobacco advertising in newspapers and magazines is a requirement to include the Surgeon General's warnings, the Multistate Master Settlement Agreement prohibits almost all outdoor advertising of tobacco, including billboards, transit ads and signs in stadiums, video arcades and shopping malls. In addition, the agreement prohibits tobacco companies from targeting youth in advertising, promotions and marketing of tobacco products, including a ban on the use of cartoons.

The alcohol industry spent more than $1 billion on television, radio, print and outdoor advertising in 1997—and total expenditures to promote alcohol are estimated to be three or more times this amount if promotional expenditures (e.g., price promotions or sponsorship of sporting events) are taken into account. Because there are no television restrictions on beer and wine advertisements, these products are promoted heavily. Ads appear at least once during every four hours of prime-time television and more than once an hour for every hour of sports coverage. Alcohol use is also shown frequently in television programming. An analysis of a random sample of prime-time television drama or comedy programs in 1991 revealed that for every hour of programming, six drinking acts occurred.

In 1997, the alcohol industry ended its decades-long, self-imposed voluntary ban on advertising hard liquor on radio and television when one company began to advertise distilled spirits on these media. Because of

Indicator 31

Billions of Dollars Spent on Domestic Cigarette Advertising and Promotion

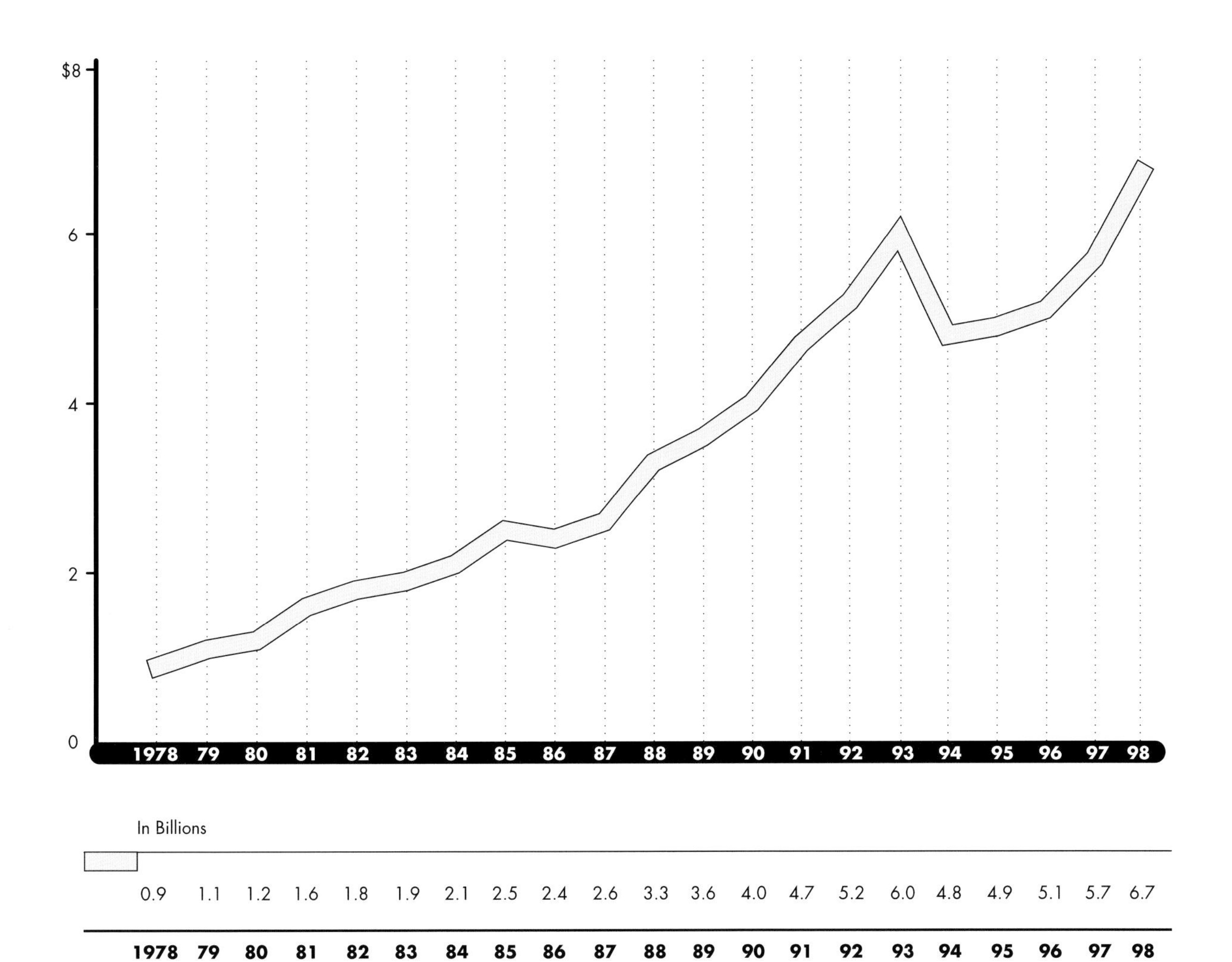

In Billions

1978	79	80	81	82	83	84	85	86	87	88	89	90	91	92	93	94	95	96	97	98
0.9	1.1	1.2	1.6	1.8	1.9	2.1	2.5	2.4	2.6	3.3	3.6	4.0	4.7	5.2	6.0	4.8	4.9	5.1	5.7	6.7

SOURCE: Federal Trade Commission. *Federal Trade Commission's Report to Congress for 1998 Pursuant to the Federal Cigarette Labeling and Advertising Act.* Washington, DC: The Commission, 2000.

concern that the rest of the alcohol industry will follow, Congress recently considered proposals to limit advertising of distilled spirits, and a 1999 Federal Trade Commission report recommended that the industry improve its self-regulatory efforts, such as barring alcohol ads on television shows and other media with large underage audiences.

Movies and popular songs—media forms particularly favored by teenagers—frequently depict alcohol, tobacco and illicit drugs (Indicator 32). In a recent study examining substance use in the 200 most popular movie rentals in 1996 and 1997, alcohol appeared in 93 percent of movies, and tobacco appeared in 89 percent of movies. Illicit drugs appeared in 22 percent, with marijuana followed by powder cocaine as the two illicit drugs depicted most often. Long-term consequences of substance use were shown in only 12 percent of films, while less than half (49 percent) of the movies depicted short-term consequences of substance use. Findings from an analysis of the 1,000 most popular songs in 1996 and 1997 revealed that 27 percent of songs referred to either alcohol or illicit drugs, and that references to substances in songs varied significantly by music category. Government agencies and private foundations are countering the advertising and media portrayals of substance use with media messages about the dangers of alcohol, tobacco and illicit drugs. Media campaigns of the Partnership for a Drug-Free America, for example, depict illicit drug use as risky to people, business and the community. However, the dollars spent on this counteradvertising are miniscule compared with the spending by the alcohol and tobacco industries.

To avoid these shortcomings, in July 1998, the Office of National Drug Control Policy (ONDCP) launched its five-year National Youth Anti-Drug Media Campaign, with an estimated $2 billion in public and private funding over this period, including $195 million in federal funding in 1998. This level of federal funding is expected to continue through 2002. ONDCP is purchasing advertising space in prime-time viewing hours for its anti-drug messages. Media outlets that accept the campaign's paid anti-drug advertising are asked to provide an equal value of pro bono public service announcement time or other activities related to youth substance abuse, including messages from local alcohol and tobacco education and prevention initiatives.

Indicator 32

Alcohol, Tobacco and Illicit Drugs Present in Popular Movies and Songs, 1996–1997

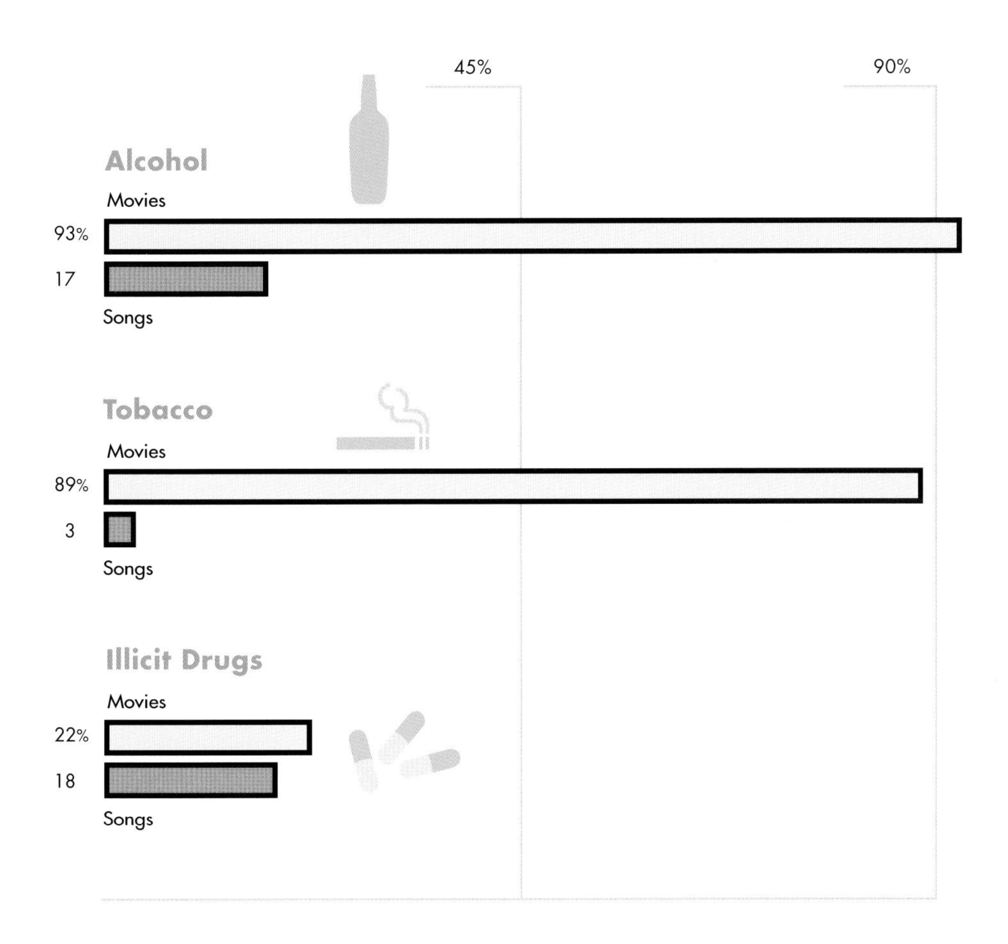

NOTES: Percentages reflect the number of movies (out of 200 total) and songs (out of 1,000 total) in which substances appeared, whether or not they were used. The sample included films with G, PG, PG-13 and R Motion Picture Association of America ratings.

SOURCE: U.S. Substance Abuse and Mental Health Services Administration. *Substance Use in Popular Movies and Music.* Rockville, MD, 1999.

Illicit Drug Control

Combating the Problem

The two major strategies to control illegal drug use are reducing the illicit drug supply and reducing Americans' demand for drugs. Supply-reduction strategies seek to curtail the supply of drugs through intercepting and seizing illegal drug shipments (interdiction), breaking up street-market dealing and other traditional law enforcement activities. Demand-reduction strategies aim to decrease the number of people who want to use illicit drugs, primarily through prevention, early intervention and treatment services. Since 1981, federal spending on illicit drug control has grown 12-fold (Indicator 33).

More money and effort traditionally have gone into supply reduction than demand reduction, although many groups have promoted a shift in this balance. Of the total federal drug control budget of more than $17 billion for FY 2000 request, the supply-reduction strategies of international and domestic law enforcement and interdiction account for two-thirds, or $11.7 billion, compared with one-third, or $6 billion, for demand-reduction strategies (Indicator 34).

In 1997, more than 250,000 pounds of cocaine, 3,000 pounds of heroin and 1.5 million pounds of marijuana and hashish were seized by the federal Drug Enforcement Administration, the Federal Bureau of Investigation, the U.S. Customs Service, the U.S. Border Patrol and the U.S. Coast Guard. Each year for the past several years, the Customs Service has made more than 20,000 drug seizures. To achieve these seizures, the federal government has made major investments in interdiction equipment, including advanced communication and detection systems.

However, despite spending more than $16 billion on interdiction and nearly $5 billion on international law enforcement over the last decade, the worldwide production of cocaine, opium and other drugs, as well as the flow of illicit drugs into the United States, remains high. Law enforcement agencies make more than a million and a half arrests for drug law violations each year. Of the total drug violation arrests, 80 percent were for possession of drugs, and 20 percent were for sales and manufacturing.

Indicator 33

Federal Drug Control Spending Rises 12-Fold since 1981

In Billions of Dollars

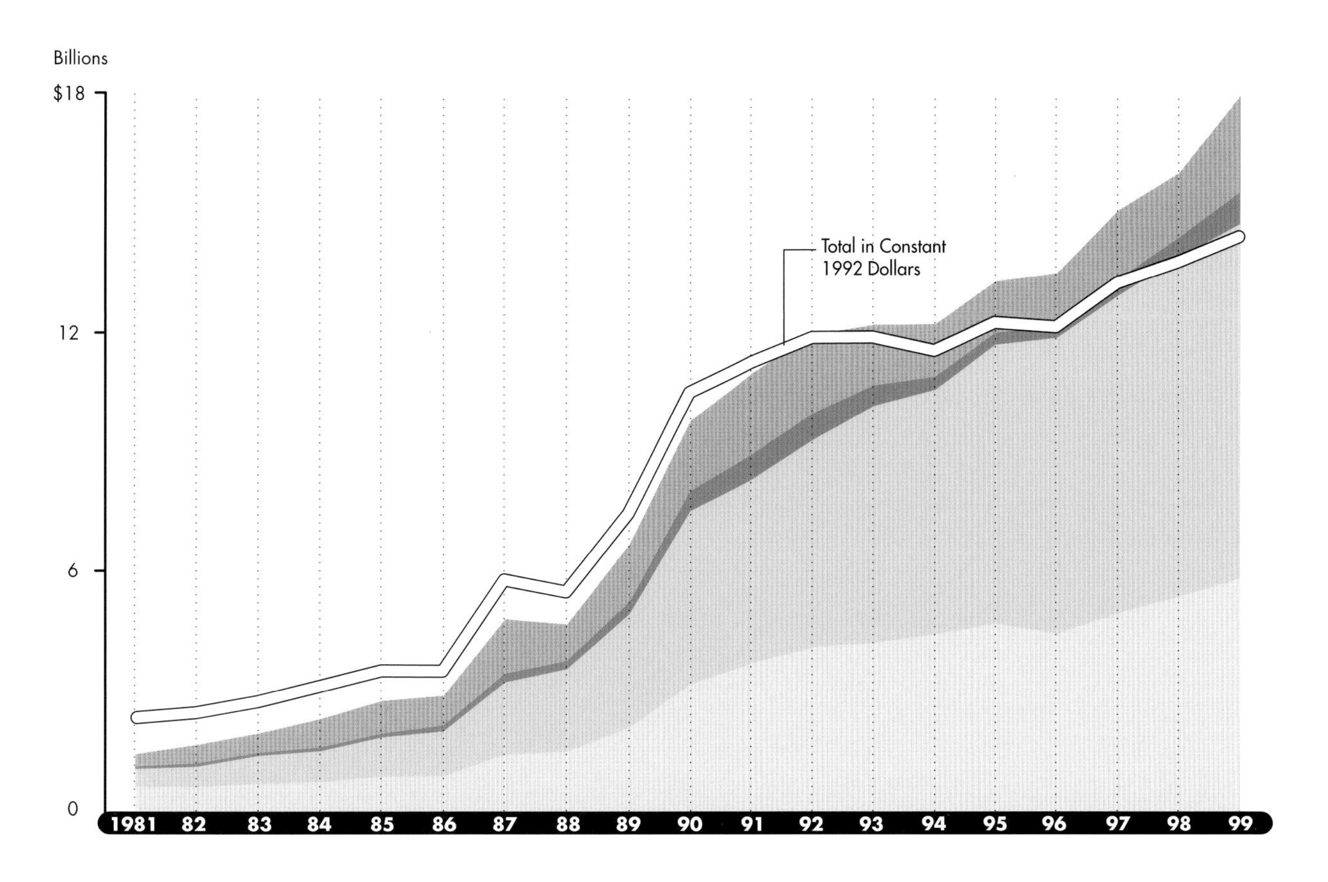

	Interdiction		International		Domestic Law Enforcement		Demand Reduction		Total
1981	$ .4	**1981**	$ .1	**1981**	$ .4	**1981**	$ .6	**1981**	$ 1.5
82	.5	**82**	.1	**82**	.5	**82**	.6	**82**	1.7
83	.5	**83**	.1	**83**	.7	**83**	.7	**83**	1.9
84	.7	**84**	.1	**84**	.8	**84**	.7	**84**	2.3
85	.8	**85**	.1	**85**	1.0	**85**	.9	**85**	2.7
86	.7	**86**	.1	**86**	1.1	**86**	.9	**86**	2.9
87	1.4	**87**	.2	**87**	1.8	**87**	1.4	**87**	4.8
88	.9	**88**	.2	**88**	2.1	**88**	1.5	**88**	4.7
89	1.4	**89**	.3	**89**	2.8	**89**	2.1	**89**	6.7
90	1.8	**90**	.5	**90**	4.3	**90**	3.2	**90**	9.8
91	2.0	**91**	.6	**91**	4.6	**91**	3.7	**91**	11.0
92	2.0	**92**	.7	**92**	5.2	**92**	4.1	**92**	11.9
93	1.5	**93**	.5	**93**	5.9	**93**	4.2	**93**	12.2
94	1.3	**94**	.3	**94**	6.1	**94**	4.4	**94**	12.2
95	1.3	**95**	.3	**95**	7.0	**95**	4.7	**95**	13.3
96	1.3	**96**	.3	**96**	7.4	**96**	4.4	**96**	13.5
97	1.7	**97**	.4	**97**	8.0	**97**	4.9	**97**	15.0
98	1.6	**98**	.5	**98**	8.5	**98**	5.4	**98**	16.0
99	2.4	**99**	.8	**99**	8.9	**99**	5.8	**99**	17.9

NOTES: The international supply-reduction strategy seeks to help source countries to reduce drug cultivation, attack production, interdict drug shipments and disrupt and dismantle trafficking organizations. The 1999 total adjusted to constant 1992 dollars is based on the 1999 request of $17.1 billion. Sums of columns may differ from totals due to rounding.

SOURCES: For 1981–1985: U.S. Office of Management and Budget, Executive Office of the President. *Federal Drug Control Programs: Budget Summary Fiscal Year 1994*. Washington, DC, 1993. For 1986–1999: U.S. Office of National Drug Control Policy, Executive Office of the President. *FY 1999 Budget Highlights: Federal Drug Control Programs*. www.whitehousedrugpolicy.gov. Total in constant 1992 dollars: U.S. Office of National Drug Control Policy, Executive Office of the President. Unpublished data.

Combating the Problem

Drug treatment gets the greater share—more than $3 billion—of the $6 billion for demand-reduction strategies in the 2000 federal drug control budget. Slightly more than $2 billion is earmarked for drug prevention and about $670 million dollars for drug treatment and prevention research. Harm-reduction efforts, such as needle exchange programs to prevent HIV infection, are another approach to dealing with problems associated with illicit drug use. Although harm-reduction policies aim to reduce the personal and social harm caused by drug use, they have often been controversial in the United States because they are sometimes seen as condoning the use of illicit drugs.

Indicator 34

Law Enforcement and Interdiction Dominate the Federal Drug Control Budget, FY 2000 Request

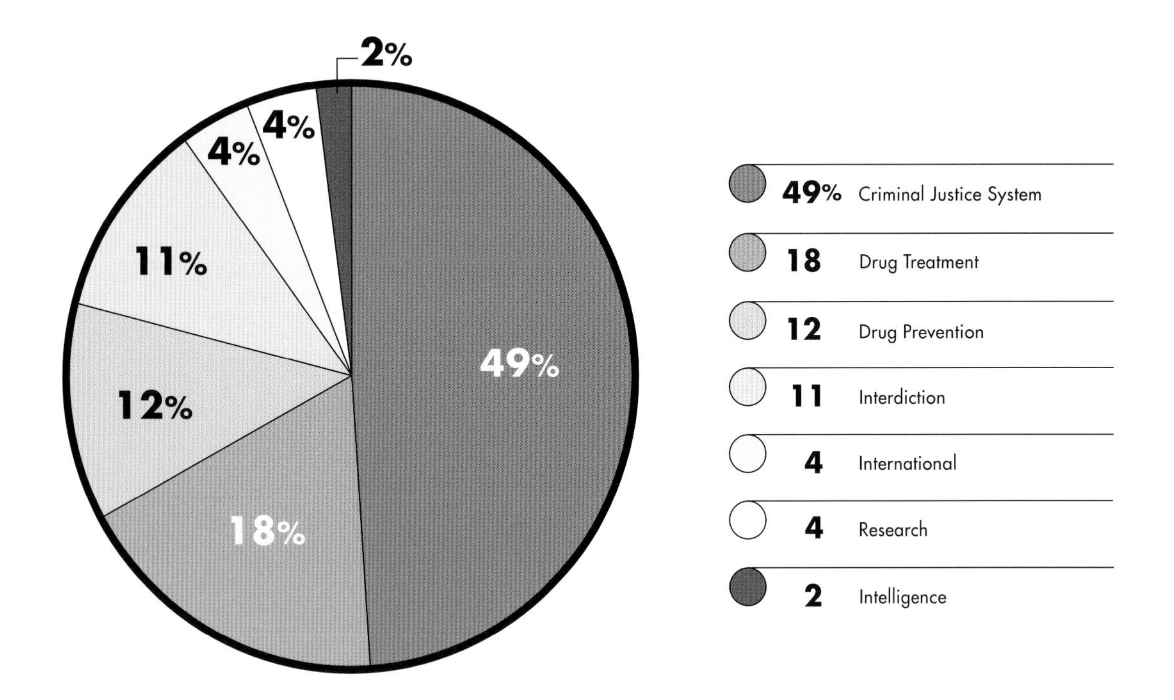

SOURCE: U.S. Office of National Drug Control Policy, Executive Office of the President. *1999 National Drug Control Strategy—1999 Budget Summary.* www.whitehousedrugpolicy.gov/policy/99ndcsbudget

Community-Based Approaches

Combating the Problem

Communities across the country continue to develop broad-based efforts to combat the problems associated with substance abuse in their neighborhoods. The focus of most community action programs is on alcohol and illicit drugs, perhaps because the problems associated with these substances are so dramatic and obvious (Indicator 35). Other programs, such as the National Cancer Institute's Community Intervention Trial for Smoking Cessation (COMMIT), have targeted tobacco use. Since 1990, the federal Center for Substance Abuse Prevention (CSAP) has provided funding and technical assistance to more than 250 communities to set up partnerships to reduce local problems stemming from substance abuse. Join Together and the Community Anti-Drug Coalitions of America, two national initiatives supported by The Robert Wood Johnson Foundation, also provide technical assistance and resources to community action programs across the country. In addition, the Foundation supports seven communities through its national Fighting Back program, 10 colleges and communities in its A Matter of Degree program to reduce binge drinking, 12 coalitions in its Reducing Underage Drinking through Coalitions program, 14 sites in its Healthy Nations program to reduce substance abuse among Native Americans and 30 states in its SmokeLess States programs.

Much coalition activity focuses on prevention and public awareness (Indicator 36) and such other activities as early intervention, treatment and aftercare. By changing knowledge and perceptions at the community level, it is believed that social norms of the community can change, too. The Fighting Back sites, for example, are working to change norms by organizing neighborhood activities to clean up graffiti and close crack houses. Many of the communities also have developed youth programs, such as peer counseling and gang prevention, and increased or enhanced access to treatment services through case management and programs to reach the underserved. Youth, college and community leaders in A Matter of Degree sites are addressing environmental factors related to alcohol use, such as alcohol prices, sales and distribution, advertising and promotion and enforcement.

Schools can play an important role in the community by educating students about the physical effects of substance use and providing drug-free after-school environ-

Indicator 35

Alcohol and Illicit Drug Use Are Key Issues for Community Coalitions, 1995

Percent of Community Coalitions Extensively Addressing Various Substances

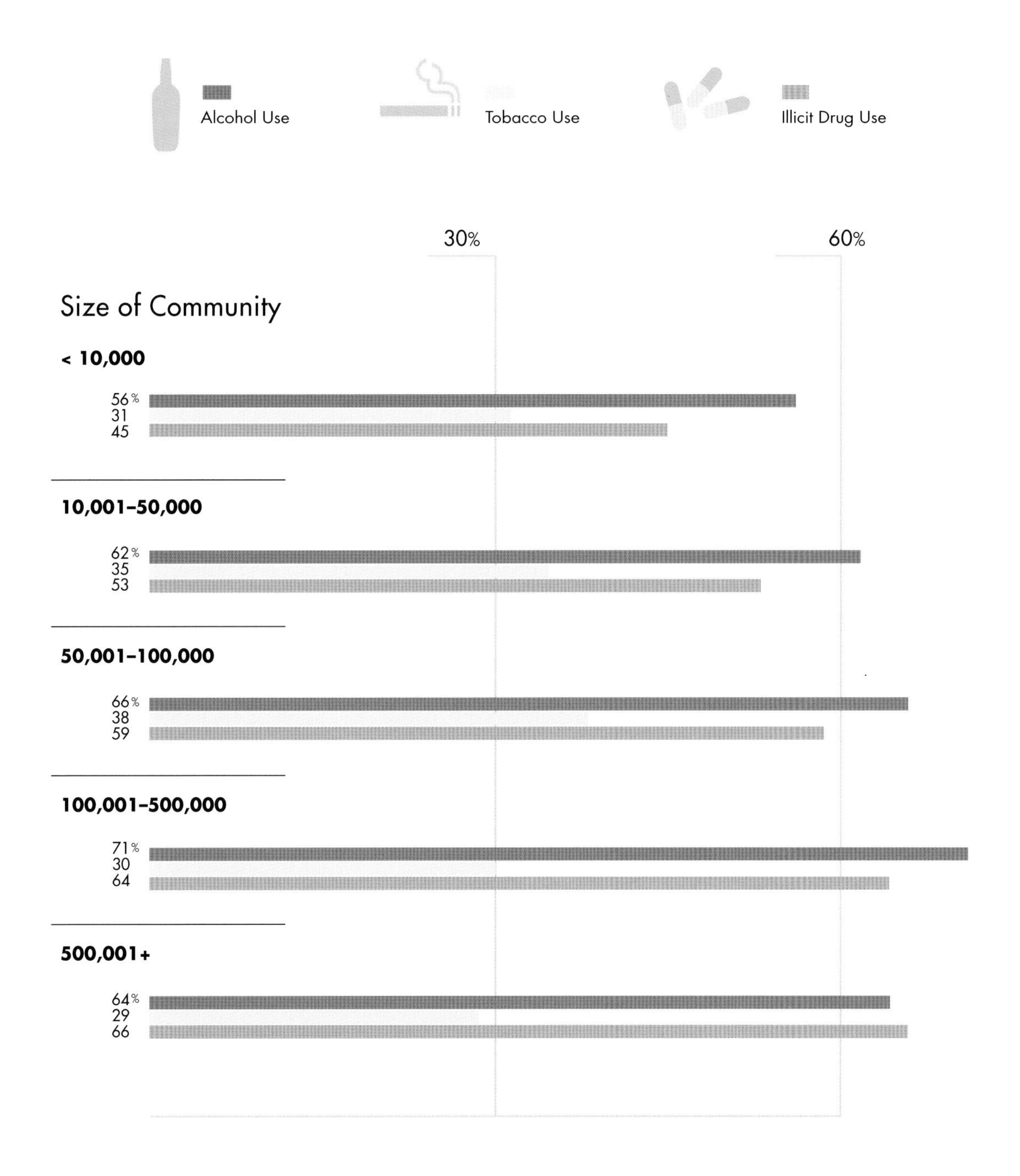

NOTES: Of the 4,177 community coalitions responding to Join Together's Third National Survey of the Community Movement Against Substance Abuse, 1,910 identified themselves as leading or sponsoring community coalitions against substance abuse. This indicator is based on the responses of the 1,910 coalitions that address substance abuse.

SOURCE: Join Together: A National Resource for Communities Fighting Substance Abuse. *The Third National Survey of the Community Movement Against Substance Abuse.* Boston, MA, 1996. Unpublished data.

ments for youth. Many schools hold alcohol-free and drug-free parties after proms and other school-sponsored events. Schools also have programs to increase student resilience against substance abuse. For example, the Life Skills Training program teaches students communication skills and stress management techniques. Other school programs educate parents about the pressures on their children to drink and use illicit drugs and how parents can mitigate them. A consistent no-use message from parents helps young people avoid alcohol and drugs. A five-year follow-up study assessing the effectiveness of the Safe and Drug-Free Schools and Communities Act (SDFSCA) showed that students in schools that had an extensive number of programs and served a large number of youth developed more negative attitudes toward drug use and a better understanding of the negative consequences of drug use, and had lower lifetime drug use.

Other community activities include media campaigns, such as those against drinking and driving sponsored by health departments and other community agencies, as well as specialized groups of committed individuals such as Mothers Against Drunk Driving (MADD) and Students Against Destructive Decisions (SADD—formerly Students Against Driving Drunk). MADD also focuses on public awareness, education, passage of legislation and federal highway funding sanctions. SADD recently revised its mission from an exclusive focus on the dangers of teenage drinking, and now also addresses other problems facing young people, including drug use, suicide and violence.

The potential impact of community-based approaches—targeting change at multiple levels within a community—can be substantial. For example, the Saving Lives Program, a community effort aimed at reducing alcohol-impaired driving, showed significant changes in the targeted behavior after five years. And after Florida's recent youth anti-smoking pilot program, which combined community-based interventions and advertisements, past month smoking rates declined substantially between 1998 and 1999 among middle school and high school students.

Indicator 36

Prevention and Public Awareness Top Community Coalition Activities, 1998

Percent of Coalitions Somewhat/Extensively Involved

Activity	Percent
Prevention	93%
Public Awareness	86
Planning of System-Wide Programs	74
Alcohol/Drug-Related Health Problems	68
Early Identification	66
Impaired Driving	60
Alcohol/Drug-Related Crime	60
Treatment	47
Aftercare	38

SOURCE: Join Together: A National Resource for Communities Fighting Substance Abuse. *Promising Strategies: Results of the Fourth National Survey on Community Efforts to Reduce Substance Abuse and Gun Violence*. Boston, MA, 1999. Table 4.

Alcohol and Cigarette Taxes

Section 3

Combating the Problem

Alcohol and tobacco use have significant external or societal costs such as higher health insurance costs to cover drinking and smoking-related illnesses, health effects of secondhand smoke on nonsmokers and the damage to life and property that results from alcohol-related accidents. While alcohol and tobacco excise taxes force consumers to pay for at least part of the economic costs incurred by drinking and smoking, current tax levels are too low to cover all external costs.

Federal alcohol and tobacco tax revenues raised over $13 billion in 1998—$7.5 billion from taxes on distilled spirits, beer and wine and $5.8 billion from taxes on tobacco. Together they represented nearly one-quarter of revenues from all excise taxes and almost .08 percent of total federal revenues. Since 1951, there have been three federal tobacco tax increases designed to increase revenue; a fourth increases the tax to 34 cents in 2000 and 39 cents in 2002. If the tax had been adjusted for inflation each year since 1951, it would be 47 cents per pack in 1997 rather than the current tax of 24 cents per pack. Factoring in inflation, today's tax is much lower than the 1951 rate. At 30 percent of the retail price, on average, the U.S. cigarette tax—including federal and state taxes—is one of the lowest in the developed world (see table).

Cigarette Taxes:
International Comparisons, 1995
Tax as a Percent of Retail Price (as of 1995)

Selected Countries	
Denmark	85%
United Kingdom	78
France	75
Germany	72
Spain	72
Argentina	70
Sweden	69
Australia	65
Japan	60
United States	30

NOTES: The data for Denmark are from 1993; the data for France are from 1994.

SOURCES: Tobacco or Health: A Global Status Report, 1997. http://www.cdc.gov/nccdphp/osh/who/usa.htm. Denmark: Brown LR, Kane H. "More Countries Raising Cigarette Taxes to Cut Health Care Costs." Worldwatch Institute Vital Signs Brief #7, May 26, 1993. Adapted from Table 1.

State alcohol and tobacco taxes vary widely (Indicators 37 and 38), and even within states the two often are not related. Wisconsin, for example, has a low beer tax and a high cigarette tax. Many southern states have high beer taxes and low cigarette taxes. State beer tax rates range from 2 cents in Wyoming to 92 cents in Hawaii, and cigarette tax rates range from 2.5 cents in Virginia to $1.11 in New York.

Indicator 37

State Beer Excise Taxes Range from 2¢ to 92¢ per Gallon, 2000

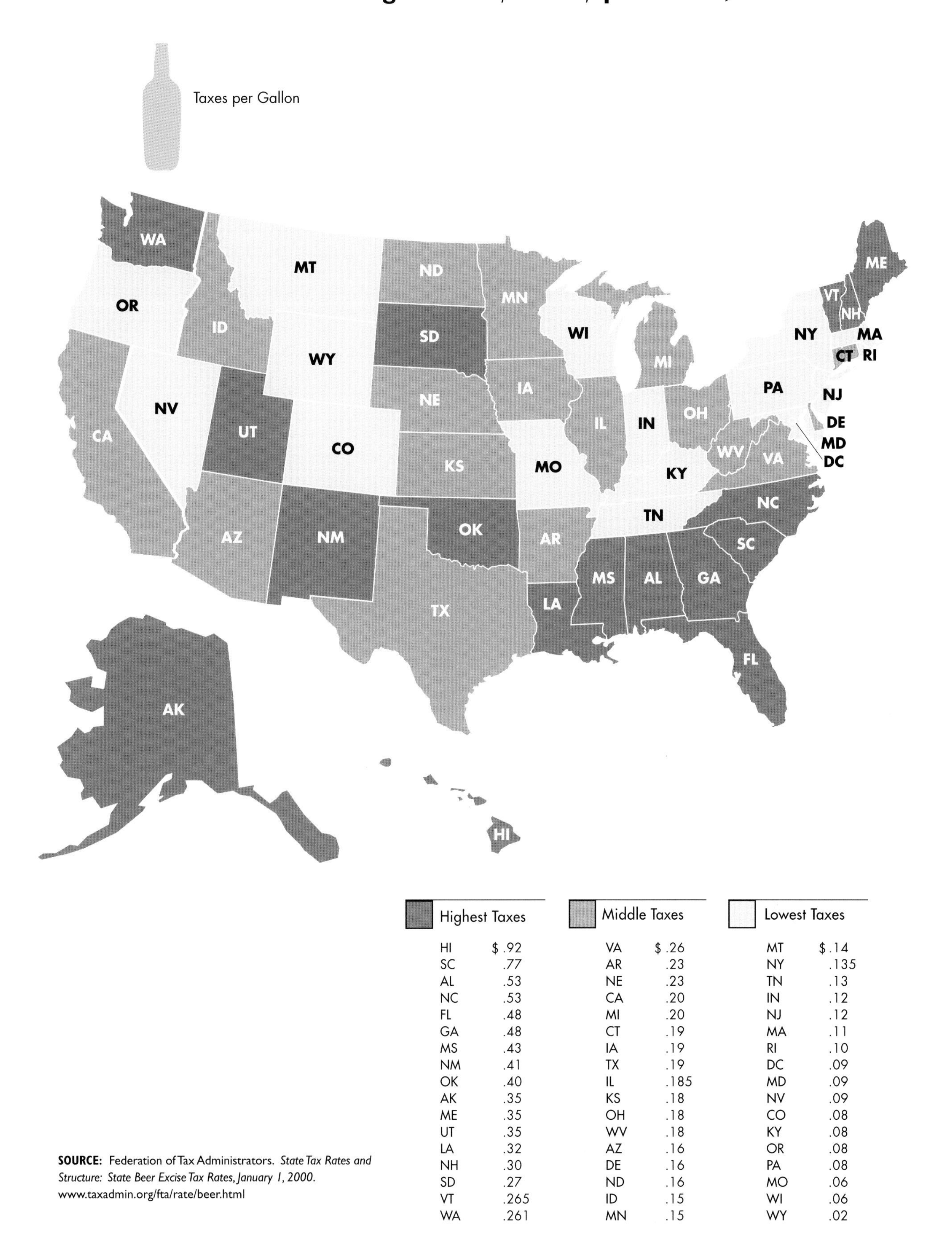

Highest Taxes		Middle Taxes		Lowest Taxes	
HI	$ .92	VA	$ .26	MT	$ .14
SC	.77	AR	.23	NY	.135
AL	.53	NE	.23	TN	.13
NC	.53	CA	.20	IN	.12
FL	.48	MI	.20	NJ	.12
GA	.48	CT	.19	MA	.11
MS	.43	IA	.19	RI	.10
NM	.41	TX	.19	DC	.09
OK	.40	IL	.185	MD	.09
AK	.35	KS	.18	NV	.09
ME	.35	OH	.18	CO	.08
UT	.35	WV	.18	KY	.08
LA	.32	AZ	.16	OR	.08
NH	.30	DE	.16	PA	.08
SD	.27	ND	.16	MO	.06
VT	.265	ID	.15	WI	.06
WA	.261	MN	.15	WY	.02

SOURCE: Federation of Tax Administrators. *State Tax Rates and Structure: State Beer Excise Tax Rates, January 1, 2000.* www.taxadmin.org/fta/rate/beer.html

Alcohol and Cigarette Taxes (continued)

Combating the Problem

Although the primary purpose of taxing alcoholic beverages is to generate government revenue, the impact of these taxes on prices affects alcohol consumption levels and related public health outcomes. However, alcohol taxes are controversial because they impose an economic burden on all drinkers, including moderate drinkers. Many people believe this burden is justified if the higher prices reduce alcohol consumption levels among alcohol abusers. In addition, even moderate drinkers may have adverse public health outcomes and impose costs on society.

Increasing taxes on alcohol and tobacco is considered an effective approach to reducing alcohol and tobacco use, since drinking and cigarette smoking are sensitive to price—i.e., higher alcohol and cigarette prices reduce alcohol consumption and cigarette sales. Researchers estimate that a 50 percent increase in cigarette prices would result in a 12.5 percent reduction in the number of smokers, or 3.5 million fewer smokers nationally. Moreover, studies indicate that youth, young adult, lower-income and minority smokers are more price-responsive than other smokers. Recent research suggests that a 10 percent increase in price could reduce the number of teenagers who smoke by 7 percent. Cigarette manufacturers have increased their retail prices recently, and the new price, plus tax increases, is expected to contribute to decreases in youth and adult cigarette consumption. These increases, however, may be offset by industry promotional discounts.

In addition to being a direct deterrent to smoking, tobacco taxes generate public revenues that can be earmarked for smoking prevention and treatment programs and health plans. Voters in California (1988), Massachusetts (1992), Arizona (1994) and Oregon (1996) approved ballot initiatives that established statewide tobacco control programs funded by cigarette excise tax revenues. Findings from Massachusetts and California show sharp reductions in cigarette sales and suggest that price constraints may be more effective when they are combined with anti-tobacco advertising and other tobacco control efforts.

Indicator 38

State Cigarette Excise Taxes Range from 2.5¢ to $1.11 per Pack, 2000

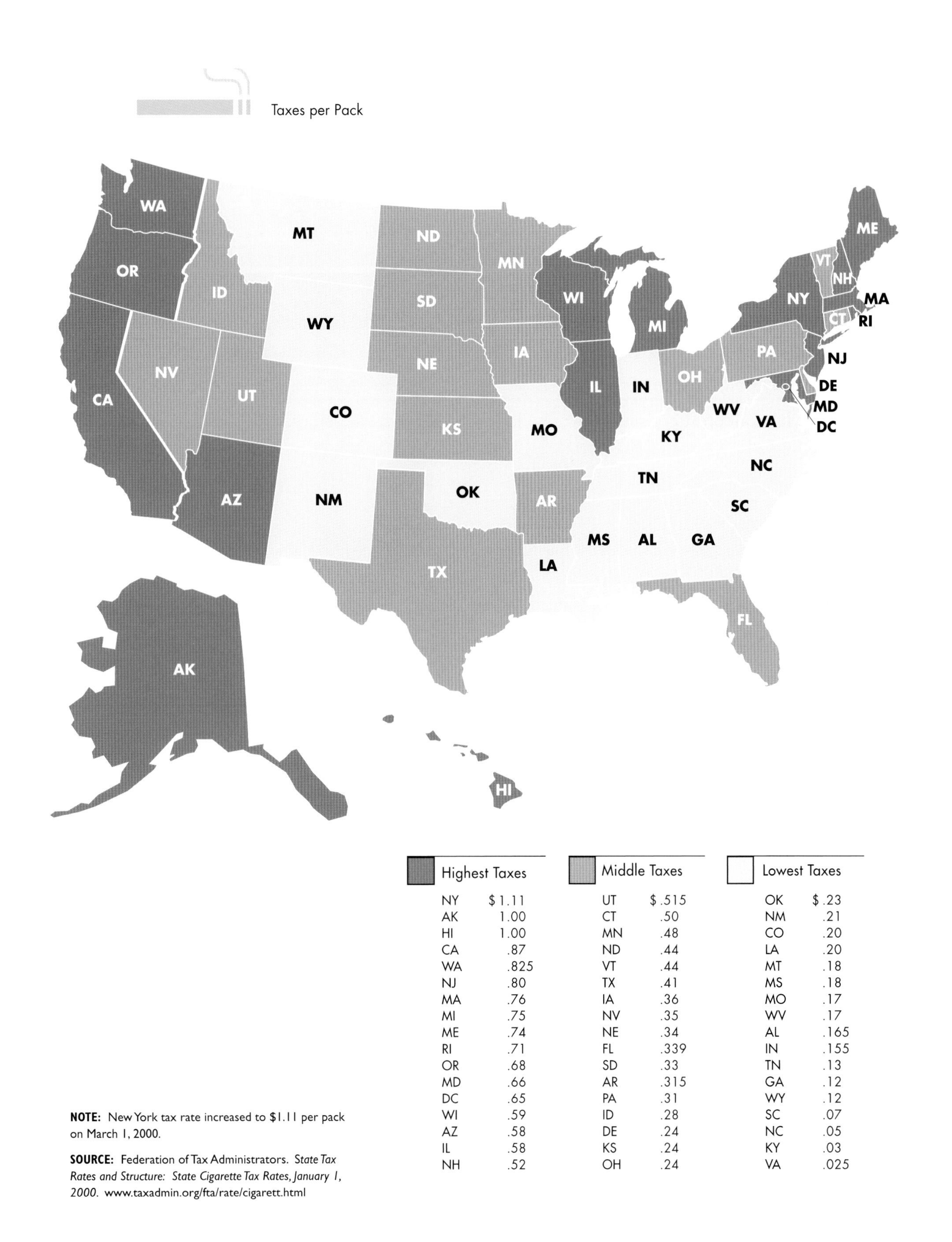

Highest Taxes	
NY	$1.11
AK	1.00
HI	1.00
CA	.87
WA	.825
NJ	.80
MA	.76
MI	.75
ME	.74
RI	.71
OR	.68
MD	.66
DC	.65
WI	.59
AZ	.58
IL	.58
NH	.52

Middle Taxes	
UT	$.515
CT	.50
MN	.48
ND	.44
VT	.44
TX	.41
IA	.36
NV	.35
NE	.34
FL	.339
SD	.33
AR	.315
PA	.31
ID	.28
DE	.24
KS	.24
OH	.24

Lowest Taxes	
OK	$.23
NM	.21
CO	.20
LA	.20
MT	.18
MS	.18
MO	.17
WV	.17
AL	.165
IN	.155
TN	.13
GA	.12
WY	.12
SC	.07
NC	.05
KY	.03
VA	.025

NOTE: New York tax rate increased to $1.11 per pack on March 1, 2000.

SOURCE: Federation of Tax Administrators. *State Tax Rates and Structure: State Cigarette Tax Rates, January 1, 2000.* www.taxadmin.org/fta/rate/cigarett.html

Restrictions on Alcohol Use

Combating the Problem

Although alcohol is a legal substance for people age 21 and older, many federal, state and local regulations restrict its use. Alcohol offenses include driving while intoxicated (DWI), public drunkenness, disorderly conduct and liquor law violations (Indicator 39). The number of arrests for alcohol offenses peaked in the early 1980s, at about 3.7 million annually (Indicator 40). In 1998, there were 2.5 million such arrests. Local laws may be challenged by the alcoholic beverage industry's promotion of preemptive state laws that diminish local control of alcohol use, such as local enforcement of minimum purchase age laws at local liquor outlets.

Despite the nationwide adoption of 21 as the legal drinking age in the late 1980s, enforcement of minimum purchase age laws is uneven. For this reason, among others, many underage drinkers are able to obtain alcohol easily—by purchasing it themselves, obtaining it from adults over 21 or underage friends and siblings or by theft from stores or parents. In one recent survey of underage youth in 15 midwestern communities, the most common source of alcohol was an adult over 21. Commercial outlets were the second most common source for 18- to 20-year-olds; a person under 21 was the second most common source for 9th and 12th graders.

It is illegal in most states for people age 21 and older to drive with a blood alcohol concentration (BAC) at or above 0.10 percent. If one drink is defined as 1.25 ounces of 80 proof liquor, 12 ounces of beer or 5 ounces of wine, a 160-pound man may be legally intoxicated at the 0.10 level after approximately five drinks, and a 140-pound woman after three drinks. However, since the relationship of alcohol consumption to legal intoxication levels is affected by many factors, including age, gender, physical condition, amount of food eaten and medication or drugs taken, this information must be interpreted with caution.

Some states have adopted a stricter drunk driving standard of 0.08 BAC. A recent study revealed that states that lowered the legal intoxication level for adults to 0.08 have had fewer fatal crashes in which drivers killed had BACs at or above the new lower limit, compared with nearby states that had not lowered their BACs. In 2000, federal legislation was signed to withhold federal highway funds from states that do not adopt a 0.08 BAC law by 2007.

It is particularly troubling that many youth drink and drive. Nearly 40 percent of 16- to 20-year-old drivers in alcohol-involved fatal

Indicator 39

Driving while Intoxicated Is the Leading Reason for Arrests for Alcohol Offenses, 1998

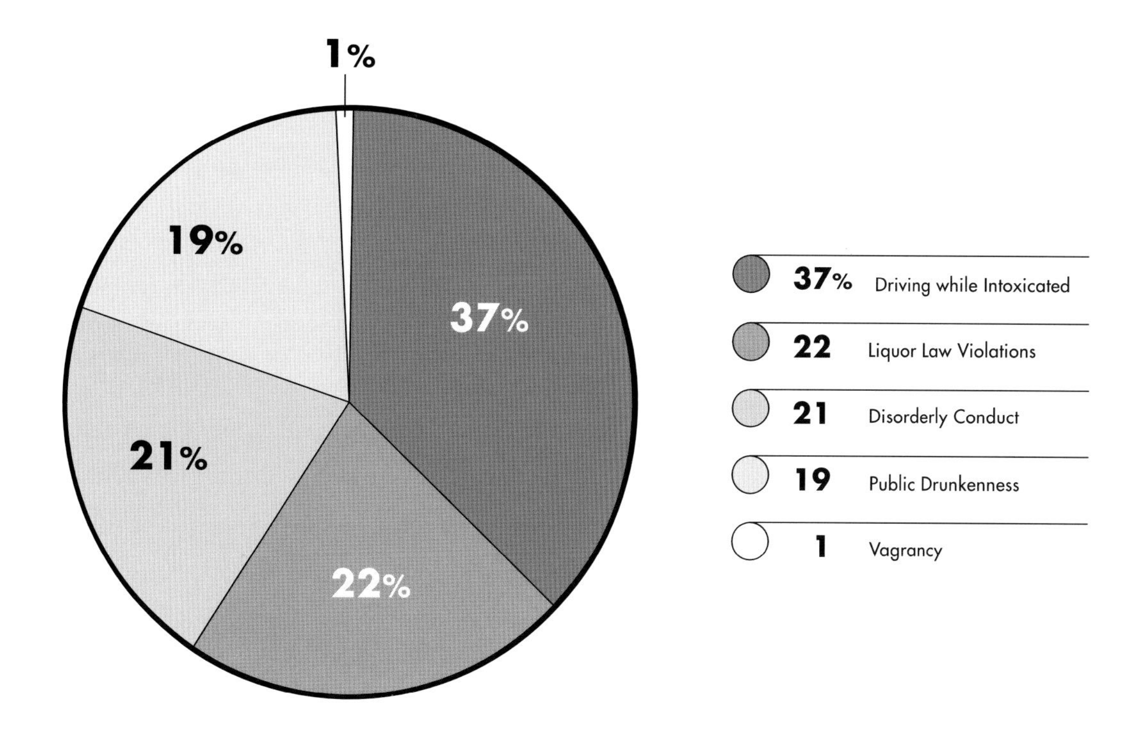

NOTE: Driving while intoxicated includes impairment due to alcohol or any other drug.

SOURCE: U.S. Department of Justice, Bureau of Justice Statistics. *Sourcebook of Criminal Justice Statistics Online*. Table 4.29. www.albany.edu/sourcebook/1995/pdf/t429.pdf

accidents had BAC levels under 0.10 percent. To reduce the involvement of young drivers in alcohol-related traffic crashes, all 50 states and the District of Columbia now have set legal intoxication levels at 0.02 or less for drivers under age 21. One recent study found that high school seniors reported less frequent driving after drinking after these laws took effect. Other studies have shown relative reductions in traffic fatalities among young people in several states that have enacted these "zero tolerance" laws compared to nearby states without these laws.

Binge drinking, a major problem on college campuses, has also received increased attention in recent years, and many colleges and universities have begun to implement alcohol policies in an effort to curb this problem. For example, more than 24 colleges and universities in the Boston area have formed the Task Force on Campus Drinking, a cooperative effort to provide support for students who need alcohol counseling, reduce alcohol advertising on campus, increase the availability of alcohol-free housing and provide other programs for underage students.

Many states hold the sellers or servers of alcohol partly liable for alcohol's consequences—for example, if they sell to an intoxicated person who is subsequently involved in a traffic accident. Server training programs may improve knowledge of safer alcohol serving practices and help servers deny alcohol to intoxicated patrons.

Warning labels have been required since 1989 on all alcohol beverage containers sold or distributed in the United States. These labels caution drinkers about the potential risks of alcohol consumption, such as birth defects, health problems and impaired ability to drive a car or operate machinery. Recent evaluations indicate that more people are aware of the warning labels, but their drinking behavior and perceptions of the risks of alcohol use have not changed significantly.

Indicator 40

Arrests for Alcohol Offenses Have Decreased since the Early '80s

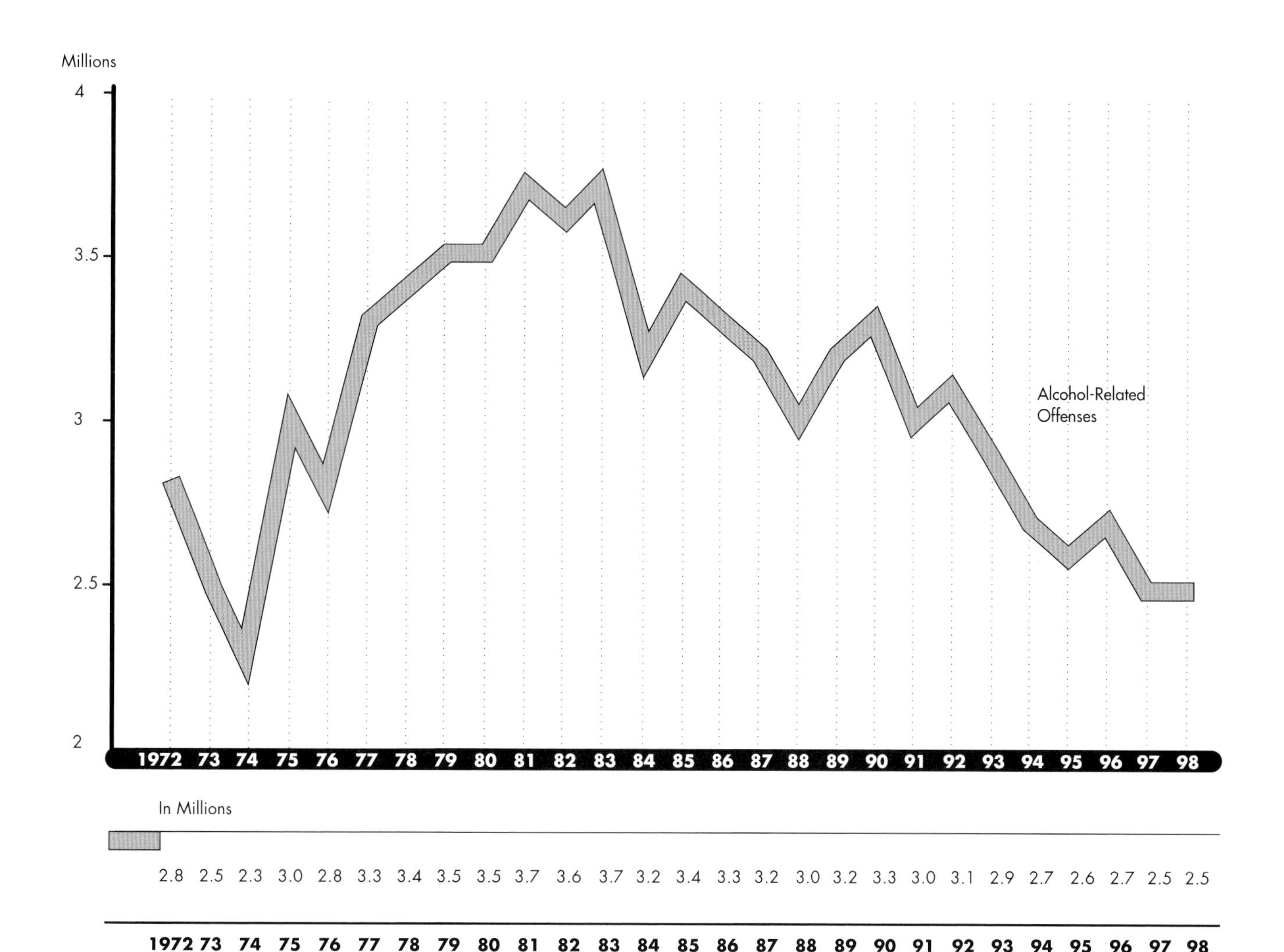

NOTES: These are conservative estimates of alcohol arrests because arrests are classified by the primary offense, not by whether alcohol was involved. Alcohol offenses include driving under the influence, liquor law violations, disorderly conduct, public drunkenness and vagrancy.

SOURCE: U.S. Department of Justice, Bureau of Justice Statistics. *Sourcebook of Criminal Justice Statistics Online.* Table 4.27. www.albany.edu/sourcebook/1995/pdf/t427.pdf

Restrictions on Smoking

Section 3

Combating the Problem

Many regulations control the sale, marketing and use of tobacco products, including a ban of cigarette advertising on television and radio. All states and the District of Columbia prohibit the sale and distribution of tobacco products to persons under age 18. State laws often penalize the business owner, manager and/or clerk for the first violation. These laws vary in their approach, however, and are enforced unevenly. As a result of this inconsistency, most young smokers are able to purchase cigarettes and other tobacco products. Underage smokers are most likely to get cigarettes by purchasing them (typically in a convenience store, gas station or vending machine) or by "borrowing" them from someone. A usual source of cigarettes varies with age, with only 22 percent of 9th graders reporting that they buy cigarettes in a store, compared with 50 percent of 12th graders (Indicator 41). Even though it is counterintuitive, more 9th and 10th graders than 11th and 12th graders are not asked to show their proof of age when buying cigarettes. Overall, two-thirds of teens in grades 9-12 who smoked reported in 1997 never being asked to show proof of age when buying cigarettes.

The 1992 Synar Amendment requires states to enact and enforce laws banning tobacco sales to minors or risk losing a portion of their federal substance abuse block grant funding. Under the Synar rules, states must create a plan for monitoring compliance with youth access laws using random inspections of a representative sample of tobacco vendors, with an 80 percent or higher merchant compliance rate with tobacco age-of-sale laws expected after several years. Although the Department of Health and Human Services (DHHS) considers all states to be in compliance with its regulations, the DHHS rules, as implemented, do not require states to enforce their laws, thus few states have implemented effective enforcement programs.

In 1996, the FDA issued regulations to further restrict the sale and distribution of cigarettes and smokeless tobacco products to minors. The rules make it a federal violation to sell tobacco to those under age 18, mandate age verification by photo ID for any tobacco purchaser under age 27, prohibit the sale of loose cigarettes and the distribution of free samples and ban vending machines and self-service displays of tobacco products in locations accessible to minors. The FDA regulations stipulate graduated penalties for retailers who sell to minors. The FDA's authority to regulate tobacco was challenged legally, however, and the U.S. Supreme

Indicator 41

Most Teens Have Easy Access to Cigarettes, 1995

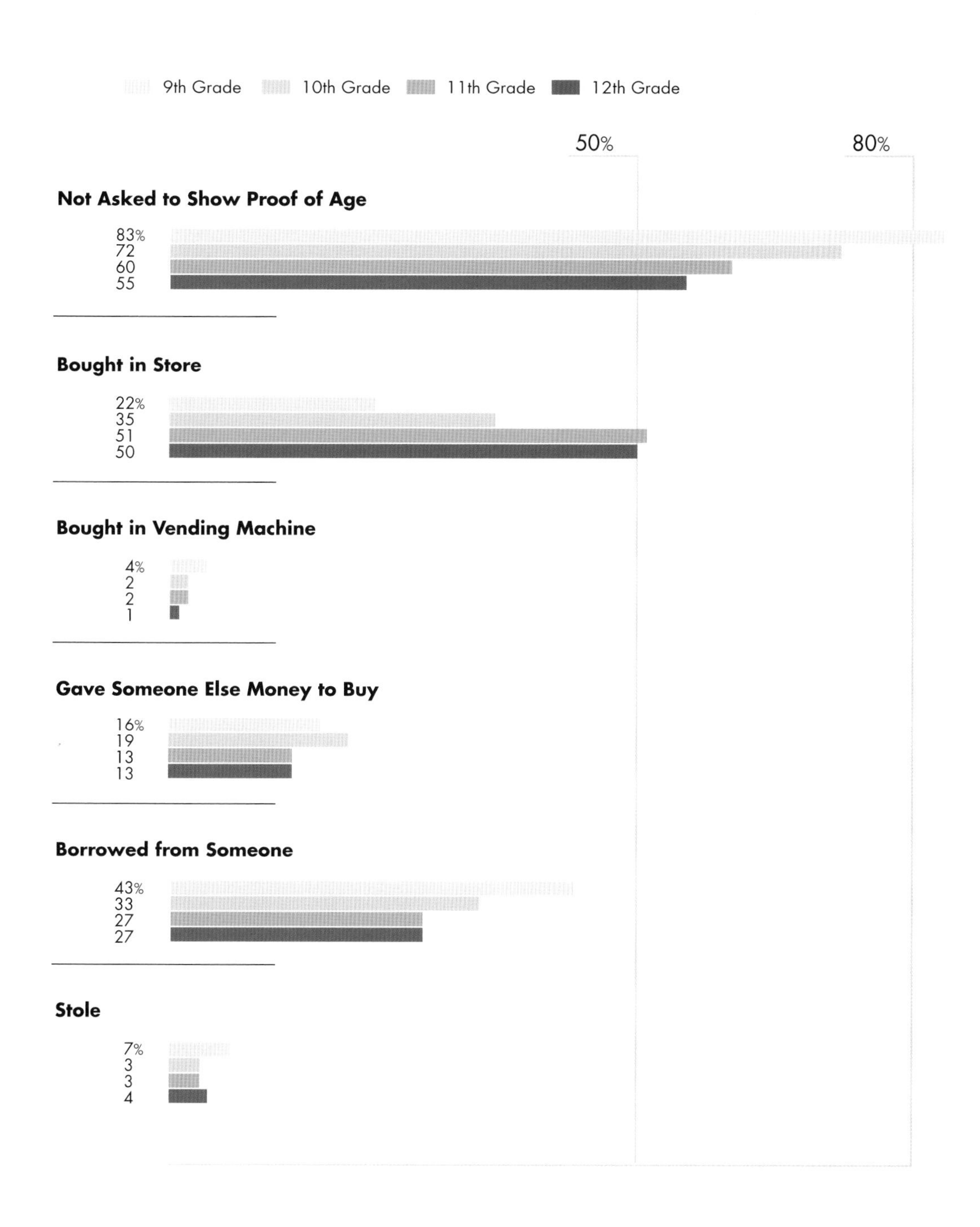

SOURCES: Data on source of cigarettes: U.S. Centers for Disease Control and Prevention. "Tobacco Use and Usual Source of Cigarettes Among High School Students—United States, 1995." *Morbidity and Mortality Weekly Report*, 45(20), 1996. Data on proof of age: U.S. Centers for Disease Control and Prevention. "Youth Risk Behavior Surveillance—United States, 1997." *Morbidity and Mortality Weekly Report*, 47(SS-3), 1998.

Restrictions on Smoking (continued)

Combating the Problem

Court ruled that the FDA does not have the authority to regulate tobacco.

More than 1,200 state laws address tobacco control issues. These laws can be grouped into four major categories: smoke-free indoor air; youth access to tobacco products; advertising of tobacco products; and excise taxes. Local laws may be challenged by the tobacco industry's promotion of preemptive state laws. Preemptive state laws diminish local control of tobacco use and limit local educational efforts and forums for public debate, which are vital to the success of anti-smoking attitudes. As of 1998, most states (30) had preemptive tobacco control laws, including 18 states that preempt one or more provisions of smoke-free indoor air restrictions (e.g., government work sites, restaurants and private work sites) and 21 states that preempt one or more provisions of minors' access restrictions.

Overall, 46 states and the District of Columbia restrict smoking in public places: 43 restrict smoking in government work sites, 31 regulate smoking in restaurants and 21 have extended limitations to private sector work sites (Indicator 42). Other restrictive laws range from prohibiting smoking on school buses and elevators to comprehensive clean indoor air laws that limit or ban smoking in all public buildings. The intent of clean indoor air laws is to reduce discomfort and health hazards among nonsmokers, but such laws have also been found to encourage smokers to quit and to reduce smoking prevalence.

Indicator 42

Most States Have Some Smoke-Free Indoor Air Restrictions, 1998

Number of States

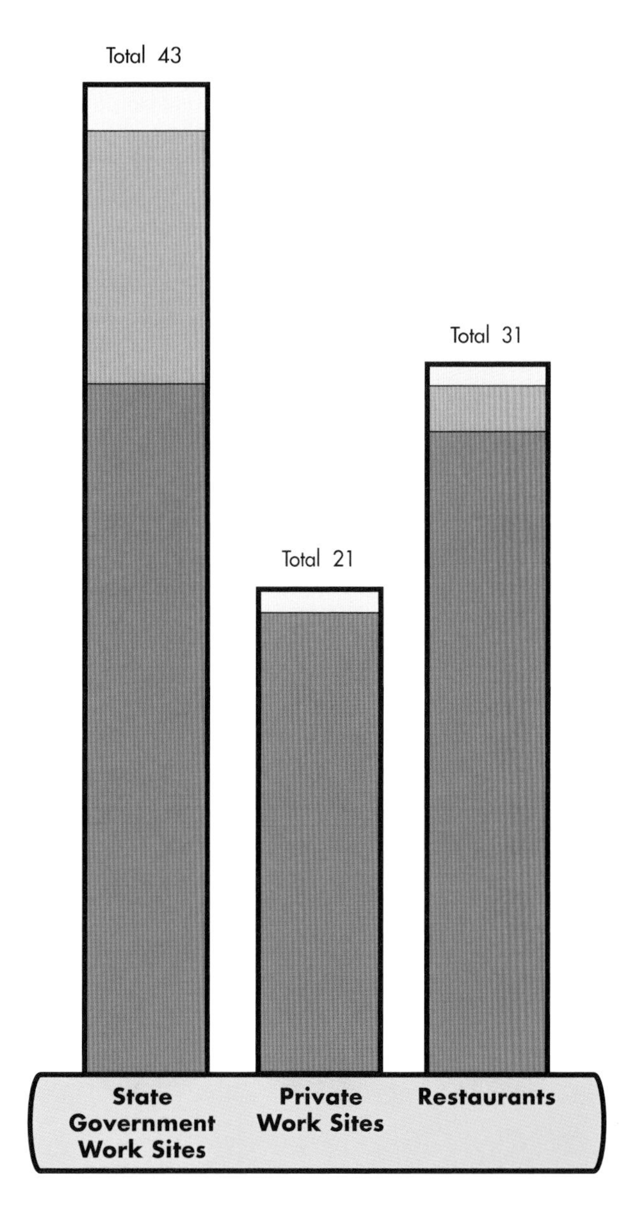

	State Government Work Sites	Private Work Sites	Restaurants
Designated Smoking Areas with Separate Ventilation	2	1	1
No Smoking Allowed	11	0	2
Designated Smoking Areas Required or Allowed	30	20	28

NOTE: Includes the District of Columbia.

SOURCE: U.S. Centers for Disease Control and Prevention, National Center for Chronic Disease Prevention and Health Promotion, Office on Smoking and Health. *State Tobacco Control Highlights—Smoke-Free Indoor Air Restrictions.* www.cdc.gov/nccdphp/osh/statehi/pdf/smokfree.pdf

Alcohol and Drug Abuse Treatment

Section 3

Combating the Problem

More than 18 million people who use alcohol and almost 5 million who use illicit drugs need substance abuse treatment. "Need" is determined by consumption patterns and the seriousness of the associated consequences. Overall, fewer than one-fourth of those needing treatment get it, for a number of reasons. For example, there may be structural barriers, such as lack of available space or limited funding, or users may not want or admit they need treatment.

More than two-thirds of the funding for alcohol and drug treatment facilities comes from public sources. Half of all funding is from federal, state and local funds designated for substance abuse treatment, and from other unspecified public funds. Medicaid and Medicare pay for another 21 percent of treatment services. A smaller portion of the total funding is covered by private insurance (14 percent) and direct, out-of-pocket payments by clients (10 percent). The remaining funding (5 percent) is from charities, donations, fund-raising events, etc., and unknown sources. In virtually all other areas of medical care, private insurance, Medicaid and Medicare—not public noninsurance dollars—pay the lion's share of costs.

There has been dramatic growth in managed care for substance abuse treatment. While this growth parallels the expansion of managed care in the broader health care environment, substance abuse and mental health services frequently are managed separately from medical services in specialty "carve-out" arrangements. In these arrangements, a purchaser, such as Medicaid or an employer, contracts with a specialized vendor for the actual delivery of care, usually through a network of mental health and substance abuse providers. In 1996, almost one-half of specialty substance abuse treatment facilities had some kind of formal managed care arrangements, and this is expected to increase as public purchasers continue to shift to managed care arrangements.

Treatment is provided in a variety of settings, and within each treatment setting a range of interventions may be available. Interventions include individual and group therapy, education and pharmacotherapy (the use of medication, such as methadone for treating heroin addiction). Structured treatment programs include those in outpatient settings, where a client does not stay overnight but where detoxification,

Indicator 43

Most People Receive Alcohol or Drug Specialty Treatment in an Outpatient Setting, 1997

Total Clients in Specialty Substance Abuse Treatment on October 1, 1997: 929,086

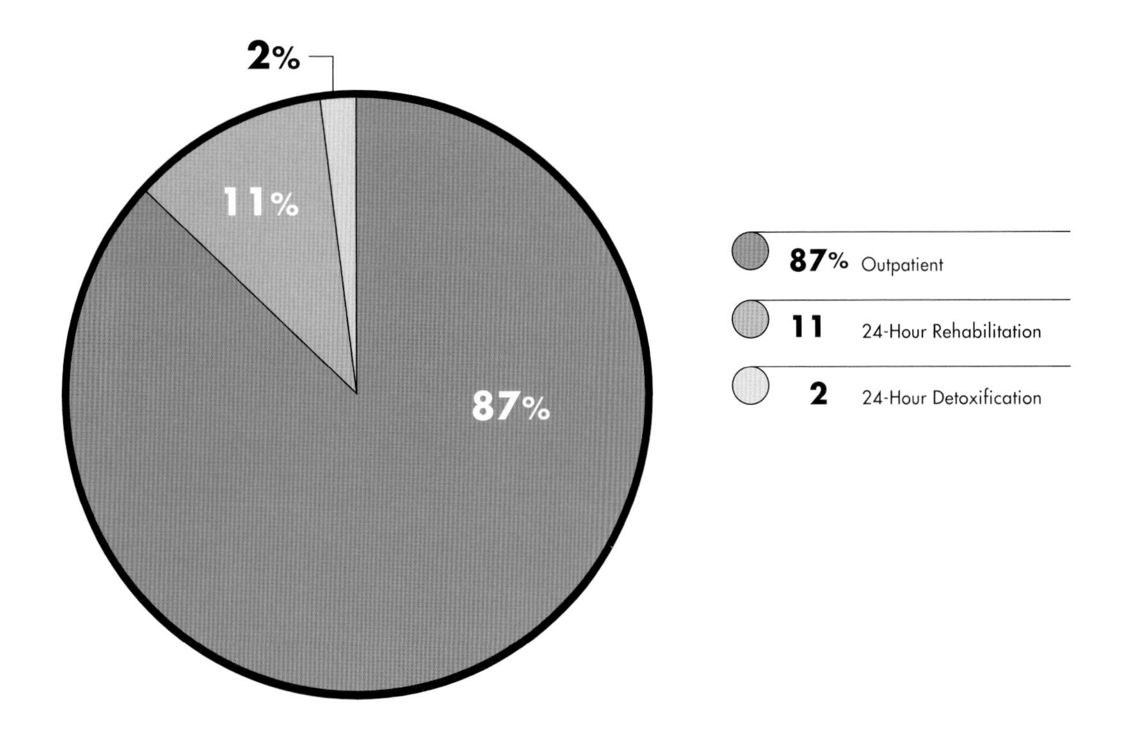

NOTES: Specialty treatment refers to treatment by public or private programs licensed or approved to provide alcohol and drug abuse treatment. Outpatient rehabilitation includes treatment/recovery/aftercare or rehabilitation services provided where the client does not stay overnight in a treatment facility; 24-hour rehabilitation includes nondetoxification hospital inpatient and residential care; and 24-hour detoxification is supervised withdrawal services in hospital inpatient and residential care.

SOURCE: U.S. Substance Abuse and Mental Health Services Administration, Office of Applied Studies. *Uniform Facility Data Set (UFDS): 1997.* Rockville, MD: U.S. Government Printing Office, 1999. p. 35.

Alcohol And Drug Abuse Treatment (continued)

Combating the Problem

methadone maintenance and rehabilitation services are provided, as well as several types of 24-hour programs for rehabilitation or detoxification services. On any given day, more than 900,000 clients receive alcohol and/or drug treatment in a specialized substance abuse treatment program—that is, in a public or private program licensed or approved to provide alcohol and drug abuse treatment (Indicator 43). In 1997, most clients—87 percent—were outpatients. After alcohol, the primary drugs of abuse for people in treatment are heroin or other opiates and cocaine or its derivative, crack (Indicator 44). The use of multiple drugs, including alcohol and tobacco, is common among people in treatment.

Alcohol and drug treatment services also are provided by family practitioners, internists, psychiatrists and other medical specialists and in emergency rooms. Physicians in these settings can provide early intervention and refer patients to specialized treatment facilities when necessary.

Self-help groups such as Alcoholics Anonymous and Narcotics Anonymous are part of the recovery process for many individuals with substance abuse problems. Due in part to these groups' philosophy of preserving participants' anonymity, accurate counts of current or former members or their current status are not available.

The criminal justice system also helps drug-involved offenders get alcohol and drug abuse treatment. Most treatment of drug-involved offenders, including DWI arrestees, occurs in the community (not in prison) and is often mandated by the court or criminal justice system as a condition of parole or probation or as an alternative to prison. For certain nonviolent drug defendants, special drug courts systematically provide sentencing alternatives that do not involve incarceration, such as mandatory court-monitored, community-based treatment and services. Fewer than 15 percent of people in prison receive substance abuse treatment, far less than the more than 70 percent in state prisons and the more than 30 percent in federal prisons estimated to need such treatment.

Indicator 44

Alcohol Is the Primary Drug of Abuse by Clients in Specialty Treatment, 1996

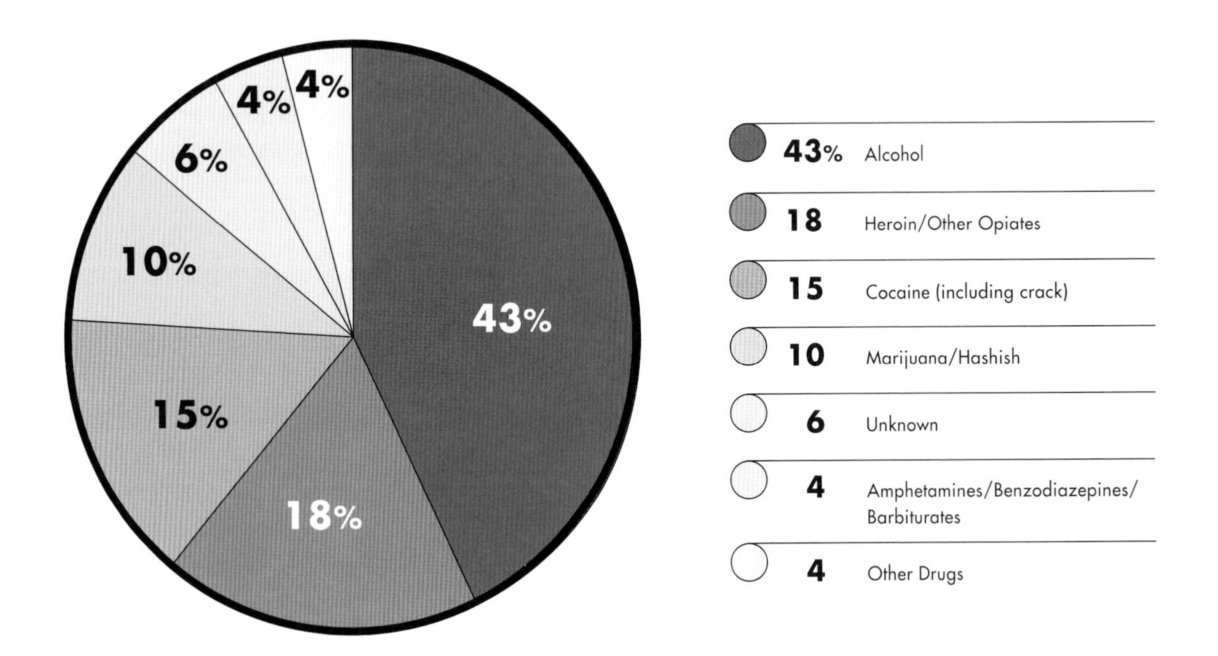

NOTES: Specialty treatment refers to treatment by public or private programs licensed or approved to provide alcohol or drug abuse treatment. The primary drug of abuse varies by treatment setting. For example, in outpatient methadone treatment, the primary drug of abuse is almost always heroin or other opiates. In other specialty settings, after alcohol, the primary drug of abuse is cocaine/crack. The unknown category exists because some facilities were unable to categorize a few of their clients by primary drug of abuse.

SOURCE: U.S. Substance Abuse and Mental Health Services Administration, Office of Applied Studies. *1997 Alcohol and Drug Services Study-Phase I. Preliminary Data.* In: Institute of Medicine. *Bridging the Gap between Practice and Research.* Washington, DC: National Academy Press, 1998. Appendix E, Table 6. p. 165.

Alcohol and Drug Abuse Treatment Effectiveness

Combating the Problem

A major question asked about alcohol and drug abuse treatment is, "Does it work?" The question is important, not only for the person being treated, but also because of the costs to society of alcohol and drug abuse. The answer is yes, treatment definitely does work, as demonstrated in numerous studies. But not all types of treatment are effective for all types of alcohol and drug abusers. And for many people, substance abuse is a chronic, relapsing health condition, so more than one treatment episode may be required before improvements, such as reductions in use or sustained remission, are seen.

Treatment effectiveness is generally measured in terms of several treatment outcomes. For patients/clients, this could mean reduced alcohol and drug use, decreased criminal activity, increased employment, improved physical and mental health and fewer family problems. For the community, these patient/client changes are related to improvements in the public's health and safety and reduced costs to society.

Treatment effectiveness is related to patient/client factors, such as severity of dependence and psychiatric symptoms, availability of social supports and the degree to which the patient/client is motivated or criminally involved. Generally, the more severe the problem at treatment entry, the worse the outcome.

Better treatment outcomes are seen in programs that provide a greater range, frequency and intensity of services and a flexible approach to individualized treatment. Time in treatment and treatment completion are also associated with better outcomes. Treatment outcome studies suggest that a minimum of several months is necessary to maintain improvements after treatment. However, the link between outcomes and length of time in treatment may reflect the fact that more motivated patients/clients remain in treatment longer.

The four most common types of drug treatment programs (outpatient drug-free, outpatient methadone, long-term residential and short-term inpatient) all reduce drug use. In the year after treatment, all four types of drug treatment programs reduced cocaine use by approximately 50 percent or more (Indicator 45); methadone maintenance reduced heroin use by about 70 percent. In addition to substance abuse treatment programs, brief interventions by doctors or pharmacotherapy can be effective

Indicator 45

Cocaine Use Drops Dramatically after Treatment

Percent of Patients Reporting Weekly or More Frequent Cocaine Use by Type of Program

Program	In the year before treatment	In the year after treatment
Outpatient Drug-Free Programs	42%	18
Long-Term Residential Programs	66%	22
Outpatient Methadone Programs	42%	22
Short-Term Inpatient Programs	67%	21

NOTES: The study tracked 10,010 drug abusers who entered treatment between 1991 and 1993, and treatment outcomes were measured using a subsample of this group. Outpatient methadone clients still in treatment were interviewed approximately two years after admission to the program. Methadone treatment is included because cocaine abuse is common among heroin addicts in these programs: about 42 percent of people who entered methadone treatment programs in this study also were cocaine abusers.

SOURCE: *NIDA Notes*, 12 (5), September/October 1997. Adapted from: Hubbard RL, Craddock SG, Flynn PM, Anderson J, Etheridge RM. "Overview of One-Year Follow-Up Outcomes in the Drug Abuse Treatment Outcome Study (DATOS)." *Psychology of Addictive Behaviors*, 11(4): 261–278, 1997.

in some cases. Naltrexone—a medication used to treat dependence on opioid drugs such as heroin—was approved in 1994 for the treatment of alcohol dependence, but it is not widely prescribed. Other pharmacotherapies for the treatment of substance abuse are in the pipeline.

Recent studies show that after six months, treatment for alcoholism is successful for 40 percent to 70 percent of patient/clients, cocaine treatment is successful for 50 percent to 60 percent and opiate treatment for 50 percent to 80 percent, with treatment effectiveness or success defined as a 50 percent reduction in substance use after six months. Other research has shown that 30 percent to 50 percent of patients/clients remain abstinent for one year after completing treatment, and that these improvements are comparable to those found in treating people for other chronic, relapsing health conditions, such as asthma, diabetes and hypertension.

Substance abuse treatment is a wise public investment and is less expensive than the alternatives, such as incarceration (Indicator 46). Numerous studies have shown the cost benefits of treatment, with reduced crime, enhanced productivity and lower health care utilization. In California, for example, substance abuse treatment generated a seven-to-one return on investment.

Indicator 46

Drug Treatment Is Cheaper than the Alternatives

Costs per Person per Year

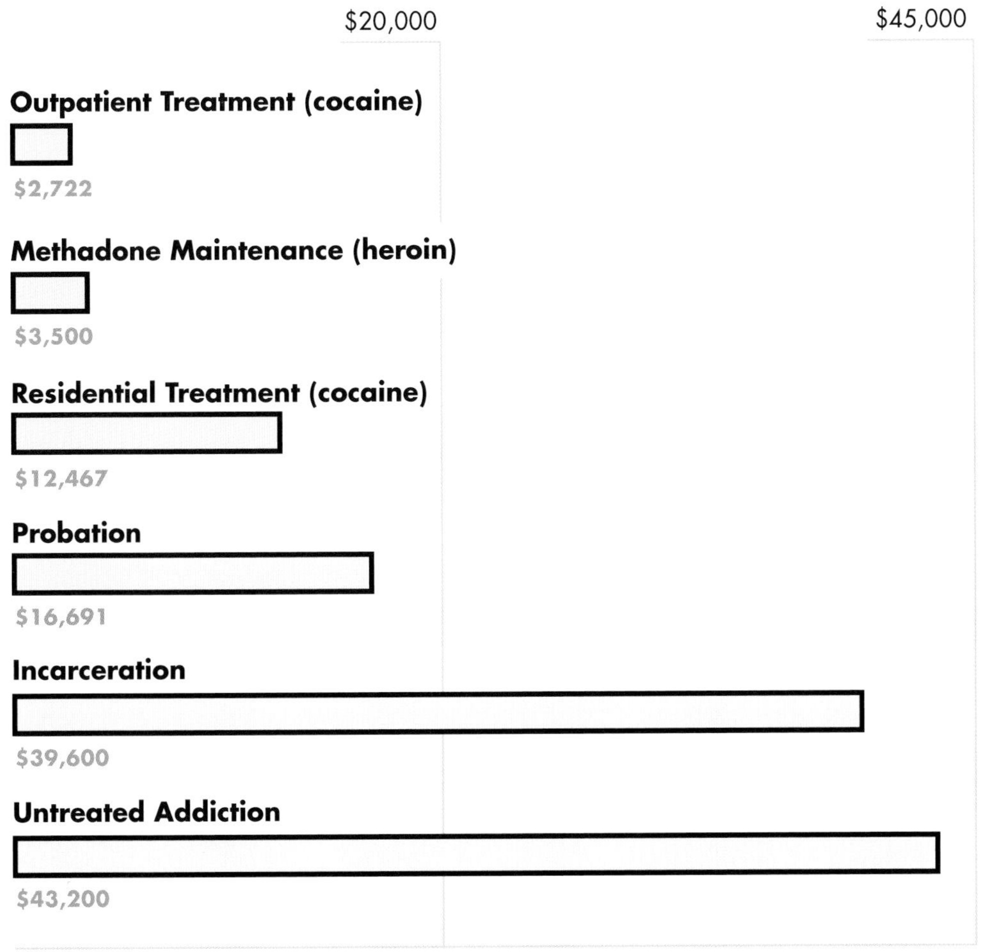

$20,000 | $45,000

Outpatient Treatment (cocaine)
$2,722

Methadone Maintenance (heroin)
$3,500

Residential Treatment (cocaine)
$12,467

Probation
$16,691

Incarceration
$39,600

Untreated Addiction
$43,200

NOTES: Untreated Addiction and Incarceration—1991 dollars; Residental and Outpatient Cocaine Treatment—1992 dollars; Methadone Maintenance—1993 dollars; Probation—1992 dollars, inflation-adjusted from 1983 data. For Residential and Outpatient Cocaine Treatment, the average cost per admission is much lower than this figure because most patients are in treatment less than one year.

SOURCE: Institute of Medicine. *Pathways of Addiction—Opportunities in Drug Abuse Research.* Washington, DC: National Academy Press, 1996. p. 199. Adapted from Figure 8.1.

Smoking Cessation Programs

Combating the Problem

More than two-thirds of the nation's 47 million adult smokers say they want to quit. But quitting is difficult, and only approximately 2.5 percent of U.S. smokers succeed in quitting each year. The most effective way to get people to stop smoking and prevent relapse is to combine proven behavioral and pharmacological treatment strategies with social and environmental support for the cessation effort.

One way to provide this support is by having a no-smoking policy in the workplace, and over the last decade, employers have increasingly instituted such policies. In 1992, 86 percent of work sites with more than 50 employees had some type of no-smoking policy, up from 54 percent in 1987 and 36 percent in 1986. Of the work sites that had some sort of no-smoking policy, 34 percent had banned smoking completely, 53 percent permitted smoking only in designated or separate ventilated areas and 40 percent offered cessation resources such as lectures and materials that help encourage employees to stop smoking. By 1993, nearly 82 percent of indoor workers in a national survey worked in places with at least some workplace smoking restrictions, and 47 percent worked in 100 percent smoke-free environments. Workplace smoke-free policies also vary by occupation. In a national survey of workers, only 27 percent of blue-collar workers reported a smoke-free environment, compared with 54 percent of white-color workers (Indicator 47). The more stringent the workplace smoking policy, the more likely employees are to quit smoking.

To be more effective, workplace smoking policies and other public policy interventions must be accompanied by programs and activities that increase motivation and skills to quit smoking. Studies show that combined treatment approaches—which include FDA-approved medications (such as the patch, nicotine chewing gum or nasal spray), clinician-provided social support and skills-training/problem-solving techniques—result in the highest long-term smoking cessation rates.

Higher-cost, more intensive treatment strategies have been found to be the most cost-effective, but brief primary care-based interventions can have a much wider reach and greater public health impact. Physician advice to quit smoking has been shown to increase long-term abstinence rates by

Indicator 47

Smoke-Free Environments Are More Available to White-Collar Workers

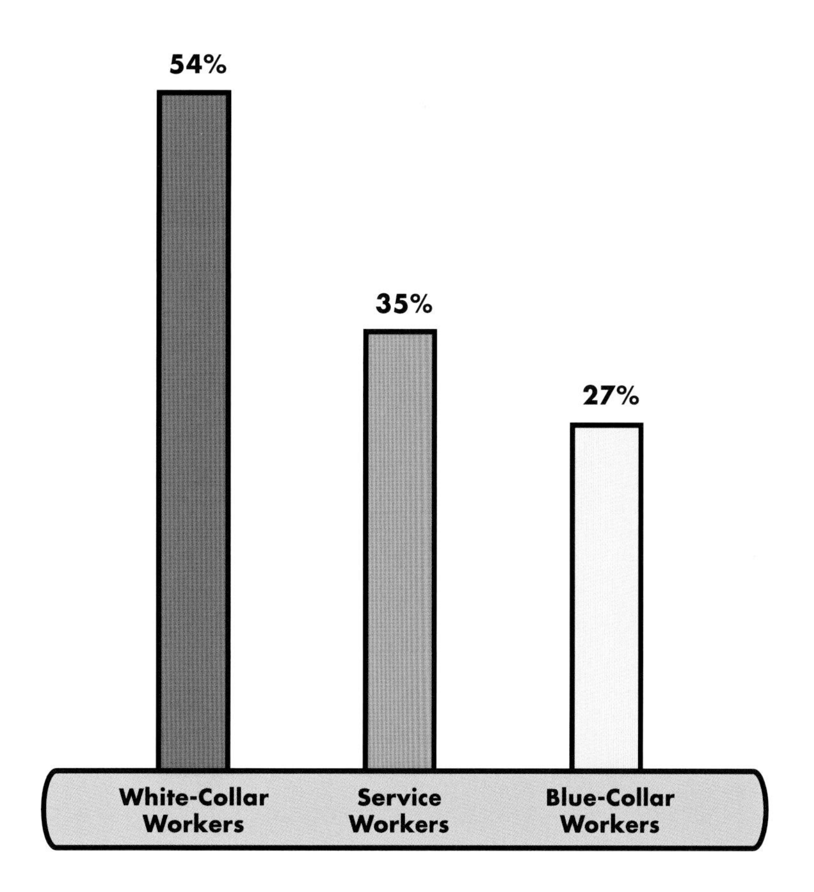

NOTES: The three occupational groups are white-collar workers (e.g., professionals and management-level workers); service workers (e.g., hotel, restaurant and janitorial workers); and blue-collar workers (e.g., skilled and unskilled laborers). Data are for 1992–1993.

SOURCE: Gerlach KK, Shopland DR, Hartman AM, Gibson JT, Pechacek TF. "Workplace Smoking Policies in the U.S.: Results from a National Survey of More than 100,000 Workers." *Tobacco Control*, 6(3): 199–206, 1997.

30 percent. Even so, health plans typically do not cover cessation services, fewer than half of all states provide for Medicaid reimbursement of smoking cessation services, and Medicare excludes such coverage. Relatively few health care providers routinely provide even brief counseling. In 1995, doctors reported providing smoking counseling at only 21 percent of office visits by patients identified as smokers (Indicator 48).

In 1996, the federal Agency for Health Care Policy and Research issued guidelines recommending that physicians and other health care providers ask patients at every visit if they smoke and if they want to quit smoking, reinforce such intentions (e.g., by helping set a quit date), motivate patients who are reluctant to quit, prescribe nicotine replacement therapy and refer patients for more intensive treatment when appropriate. Fewer than half of all managed care plans surveyed in 1997 that had reviewed the guidelines reported even partially implementing the recommendations, and only 75 percent of all plans reported any coverage for smoking cessation interventions, most often for self-help materials and least often for medication.

The growth of managed care, with its strong incentives to control costs through illness prevention, combined with the new clinical practice guidelines, may increase the rate of primary care smoking cessation counseling and treatment. In addition, one of the new performance measures for managed care plans established by the National Committee for Quality Assurance (NCQA) examines the percentage of adult smokers who have been advised by a health care professional to quit. In fact, recent evidence suggests that this measure may increase provider quitting assistance.

Indicator 48

Few Doctors Counsel Patients about Smoking Cessation

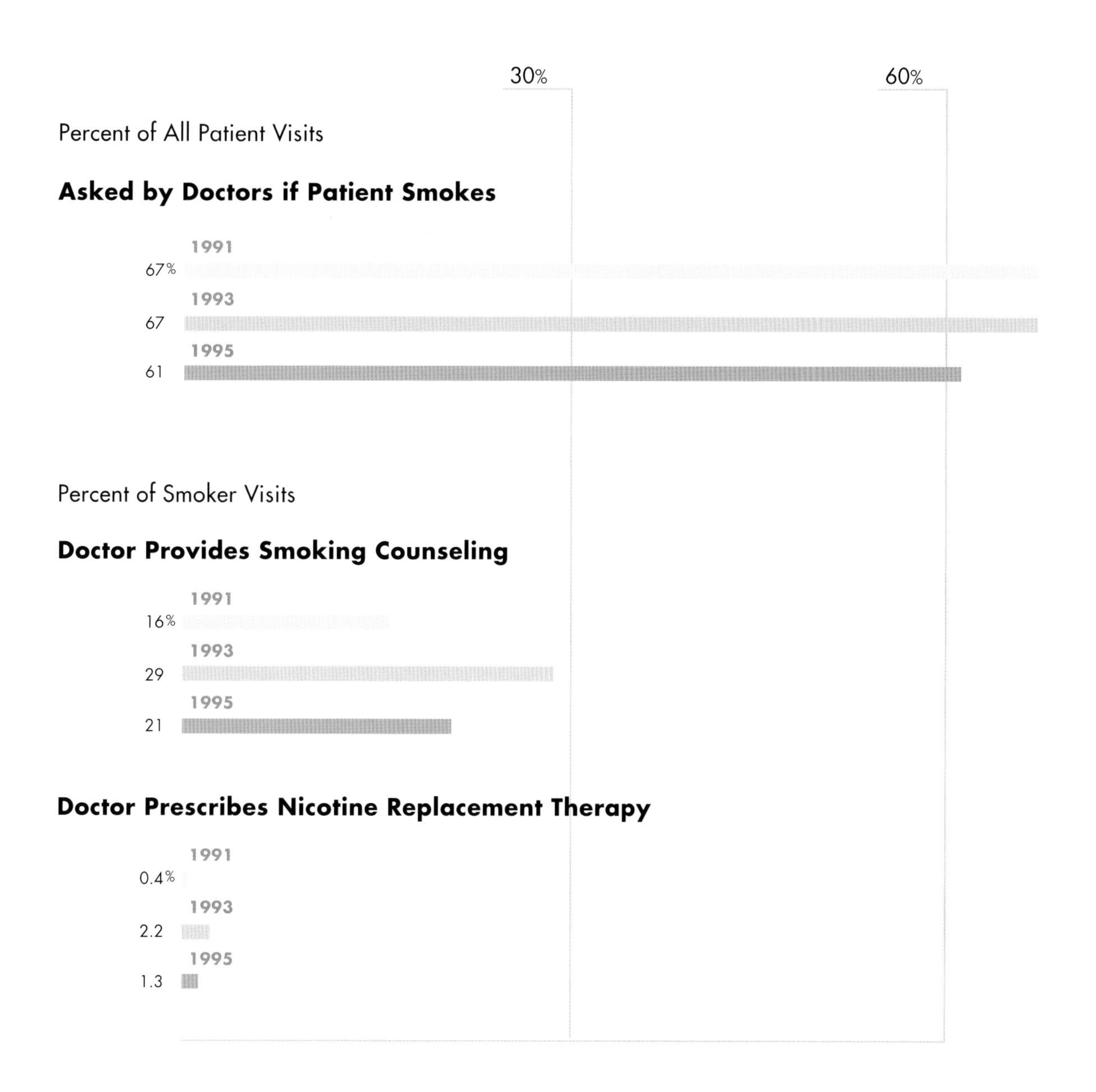

NOTE: Analysis conducted on visits to physicians by patients age 18 and older.

SOURCE: Thorndike AN, Rigotti NA, Stafford RS, Singer DE. "National Patterns in the Treatment of Smokers by Physicians." *JAMA*, 279(8): 604–608, 1998.

Combating the Problem

PUBLIC ATTITUDES

Gallup Organization. *Consult with America: A Look at How Americans View the Country's Drug Problem.* Rockville, MD: Office of National Drug Control Policy, 1996.

U.S. Department of Justice, Bureau of Justice Statistics. *Sourcebook of Criminal Justice Statistics, 1998.* Washington, DC, 1999.

THE MEDIA

Martin SE and Mail PD. *The Effects of the Mass Media on the Use and Abuse of Alcohol.* National Institute on Alcohol Abuse and Alcoholism, Research Monograph No. 28. Bethesda, MD, 1995.

Saffer H. "Studying the Effects of Alcohol Advertising on Consumption." *Alcohol Health and Research World,* 20(4): 266–272, 1996.

U.S. Substance Abuse and Mental Health Services Administration. *Substance Use in Popular Movies and Music.* Rockville, MD, 1999.

ILLICIT DRUG CONTROL

Office of National Drug Control Policy, Executive Office of the President. *The National Drug Control Strategy, 2000.* Washington, DC, 2000.

COMMUNITY-BASED APPROACHES

Aguirre-Molina M and Gorman DM. "Community-Based Approaches for the Prevention of Alcohol, Tobacco and Other Drug Uses." *Annual Review of Public Health,* 17: 337–358, 1996.

Winick C and Larson MJ. "Community-Based Prevention and Education." In Lowinson JH (ed.) *Substance Abuse: A Comprehensive Textbook.* Philadelphia: William & Wilkins, 1997.

ALCOHOL AND CIGARETTE TAXES

Grossman M and Chaloupka FJ. "Cigarette Taxes: The Straw to Break the Camel's Back." *Public Health Reports,* 112: 291–297, 1997.

Kenkel D and Manning W. "Perspectives on Alcohol Taxation." *Alcohol Health and Research World,* 20(4): 230–238, 1996.

Meier KJ and Licari MJ. "The Effect of Cigarette Taxes on Cigarette Consumption, 1955 through 1994." *American Journal of Public Health,* 87(7): 1126–1130, 1997.

Siegel M and Biener L. "Evaluating the Impact of Statewide Anti-Tobacco Campaigns: The Massachusetts and California Tobacco Control Programs." *Journal of Social Issues,* 53(1): 147–168, 1997.

RESTRICTIONS ON ALCOHOL USE

Hingson R, Hereen T and Winter M. "Lower Legal Blood Alcohol Limits for Young Drivers." *Public Health Reports* 109(6): 738–744, 1994.

National Institute on Alcoholism and Alcohol Abuse, *Preventing Alcohol Abuse and Related Problems.* Alcohol Alert, No. 34, 1996.

Pacific Institute for Research and Evaluation. *Strategies to Reduce Underage Alcohol Use: Typology and Brief Overview.* Report prepared for the U.S. Department of Justice Office of Juvenile Justice and Delinquency Prevention, June 1999.

RESTRICTIONS ON SMOKING

U.S. Centers for Disease Control and Prevention. "State Laws on Tobacco Control—United States, 1995." *Morbidity and Mortality Weekly Report,* 44(SS-6), 1995.

U.S. Centers for Disease Control and Prevention. "Tobacco Use and Usual Source of Cigarettes Among High School Students—United States, 1995." *Morbidity and Mortality Weekly Report,* 45(20), 1996.

U.S. Centers for Disease Control and Prevention, National Center for Chronic Disease Prevention and Health Promotion and the Office on Smoking and Health. *State Tobacco Control Highlights—1996.* Atlanta, GA, 1996.

ALCOHOL AND DRUG ABUSE TREATMENT

Horgan, C. "Need and Access to Drug Abuse Treatment." In Egertson JA, Fox DM, Leshner AI (eds.) *Treating Drug Abusers Effectively.* Malden, MA: Blackwell Publishers, 1997.

Institute of Medicine. *Managing Managed Care: Quality Improvement in Behavioral Health.* Washington, DC: National Academy Press, 1997.

Institute of Medicine. *Pathways of Addiction: Opportunities in Drug Abuse Research.* Washington, DC: National Academy Press, 1996.

U.S. Substance Abuse and Mental Health Services Administration, Office of Applied Studies. *Uniform Facility Data Set (UFDS): Data for 1995 and 1980–1995.* Rockville, MD, 1997.

ALCOHOL AND DRUG ABUSE TREATMENT EFFECTIVENESS

Hubbard RL, Craddock SG, Flynn RM, Anderson J and Etheridge RM. "Overview of 1-Year Follow-up Outcomes in the Drug Abuse Treatment Outcome Study (DATOS). *Psychology of Addictive Behaviors,* 11(4): 261–278, 1997.

McLellan AT, Woody GE, Metzger D, McKay J, Durell J, Alterman AI and O'Brien CP. "Evaluating the Effectiveness of Addiction Treatments: Reasonable Expectations, Appropriate Comparisons." In Egertson JA, Fox DM, Leshner AI (eds.). *Treating Drug Abusers Effectively.* Malden, MA: Blackwell Publishers, 1997.

U.S. Substance Abuse and Mental Health Services Administration, Office of Applied Studies. *Overview of Addiction Treatment Effectiveness.* Rockville, MD, 1995.

SMOKING CESSATION PROGRAMS

"AHCPR Smoking Cessation Guideline: Its Goals and Impact." Proceedings of a National United States Conference Convened by the Society for Research on Nicotine and Tobacco. *Tobacco Control,* 6(Supp. 1): S1–S106, 1997.

Orleans CT. "Treating Nicotine Dependence in Medical Settings: A Stepped-Care Model." In Orleans CT, Slade J. (eds.). *Nicotine Addiction: Principles and Management.* New York: Oxford University Press, 1993.

U.S. Department of Health and Human Services. *Reducing Tobacco Use: A Report of the Surgeon General.* Atlanta, GA: Centers for Disease Control and Prevention, National Center for Chronic Disease and Health Promotion, Office on Smoking and Health, 2000.

Conclusion

Substance Abuse: The Nation's Number One Health Problem documents the devastating impact that alcohol, tobacco and illicit drug use have on our society. These findings present clearly defined challenges that must be met in the 21st century.

While overall rates of substance use are declining, and public intolerance of abuse is rising, some disturbing trends are on the horizon. Adolescents are starting to use alcohol, tobacco and illicit drugs at increasingly younger ages, and young adults—just when they are beginning to assume more mature responsibilities in society—are more likely than other age groups to drink heavily, smoke cigarettes and use illicit drugs. And clusters of substance use—often multiple substances—are emerging among people with low incomes. Awareness of these trends will help public health educators and health policy makers as they plan prevention, intervention and treatment strategies.

Numerous studies document the success of substance abuse treatment. With the increased knowledge base about substance abuse and addiction, new treatment possibilities are on the horizon. In the 21st century, there will be more comprehensive approaches to treat alcohol and illicit drug use and to help smokers quit. The best treatment programs combine behavioral and pharmacological treatments with other social services (e.g., medical, child care and vocational) designed to address individual needs.

Many communities across the country have taken positive steps to combat the problem of substance abuse. From large cities to rural America, prevention, intervention and treatment activities are ongoing. Alcohol- and drug-free school parties, smoke-free buildings and drug courts are becoming more common. The trends noted in this report will provide useful benchmarks for assessing the impact of these efforts and, ultimately, for changing the picture of substance abuse in the United States.

Appendices

Appendix A

Selected Substance Abuse-Related Web Sites

Alcohol-Related Injury and Violence Literature Database
www.andornot.com/trauma

Centers for Disease Control and Prevention (CDC)
www.cdc.gov

Center for Substance Abuse Research (CESAR), University of Maryland
www.cesar.umd.edu

Drug Strategies
www.drugstrategies.org

The Gallup Organization
www.gallup.com

Impacteen
www.uic.edu/orgs/impacteen

Join Together
www.jointogether.org

Monitoring the Future Study, University of Michigan
www.isr.umich.edu/src/mtf/

Mothers Against Drunk Driving (MADD)
www.madd.org

National Center on Addiction and Substance Abuse at Columbia University (CASA)
www.casacolumbia.org

National Institute on Alcohol Abuse and Alcoholism (NIAAA)
www.niaaa.nih.gov

National Institute on Drug Abuse (NIDA)
www.nida.nih.gov

Office of National Drug Control Policy (ONDCP)
www.whitehousedrugpolicy.gov

Partnership for a Drug-Free America (PDFA)
www.drugfreeamerica.org

Research Institute on Addictions (RIA)
www.ria.org

The Robert Wood Johnson Foundation Substance Abuse Policy Research Program
www.rwjf.org

Smoke-Free Families
www.smokefreefamilies.uab.edu

The Smoker's Quitline
www.quitnet.org

Substance Abuse and Mental Health Services Administration (SAMHSA)
www.samhsa.gov

Appendix B

Progress on Selected Objectives in *Healthy People 2000*: Alcohol and Other Drugs

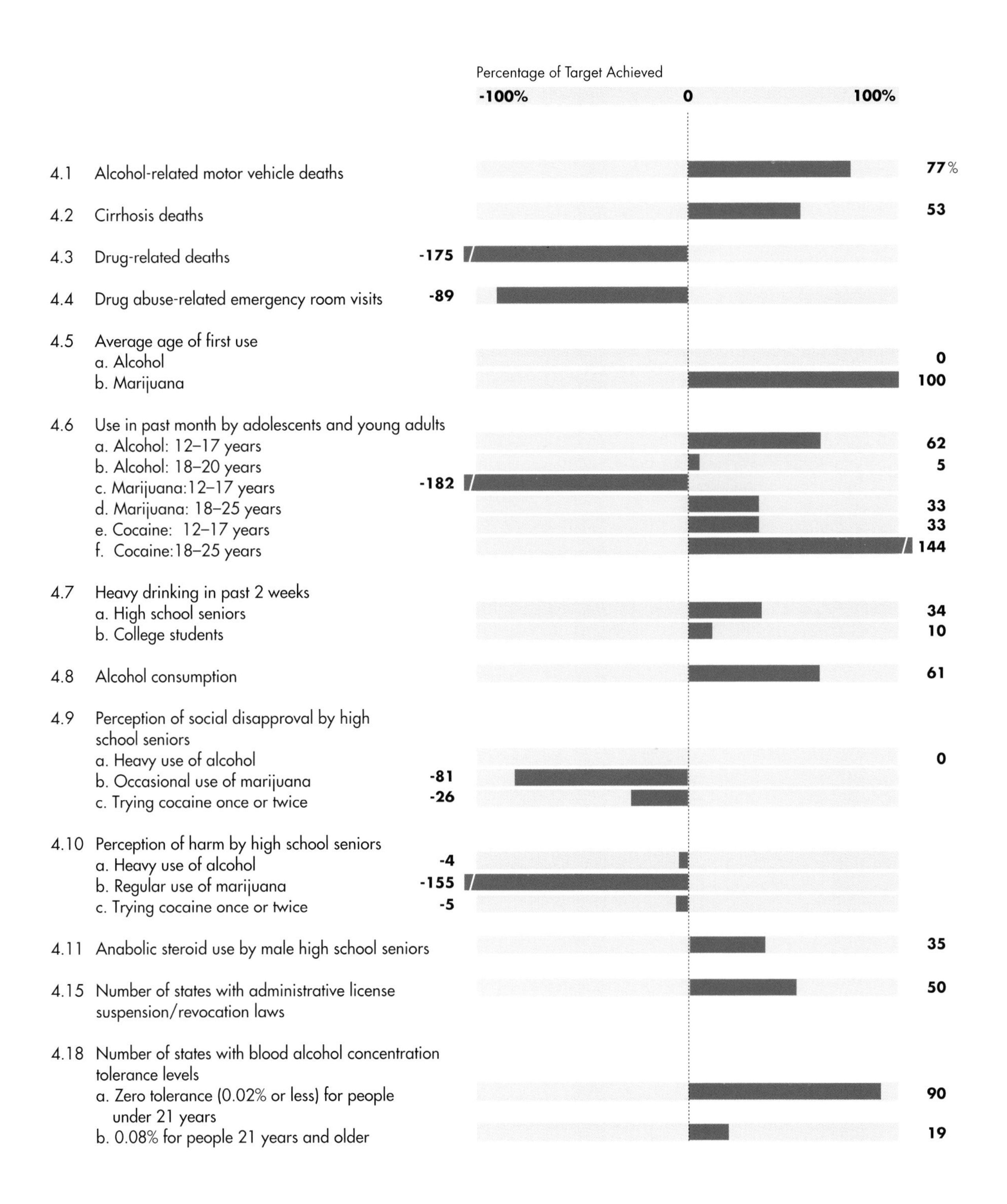

NOTES: The percentage of target achieved was 0 percent for objectives 4.5a and 4.9a. The percentage of target achieved was not calculated for every alcohol- or drug-related objective. In 1990, the Department of Health and Human Services released its *Healthy People 2000* objectives, including those related to the use of tobacco, alcohol and other drugs, with the goal of improving the health of Americans by the end of the century. These charts report on the nation's progress toward these objectives, comparing baseline data from the 1990 report with the most recent data available by the end of 1999.

SOURCE: National Center for Health Statistics. *Healthy People 2000 Review, 1998–1999*. Hyattsville, MD: Public Health Service, 1999. Chart adapted by Brandeis staff.

Appendix C

Progress on Selected Objectives in *Healthy People 2000*: Tobacco

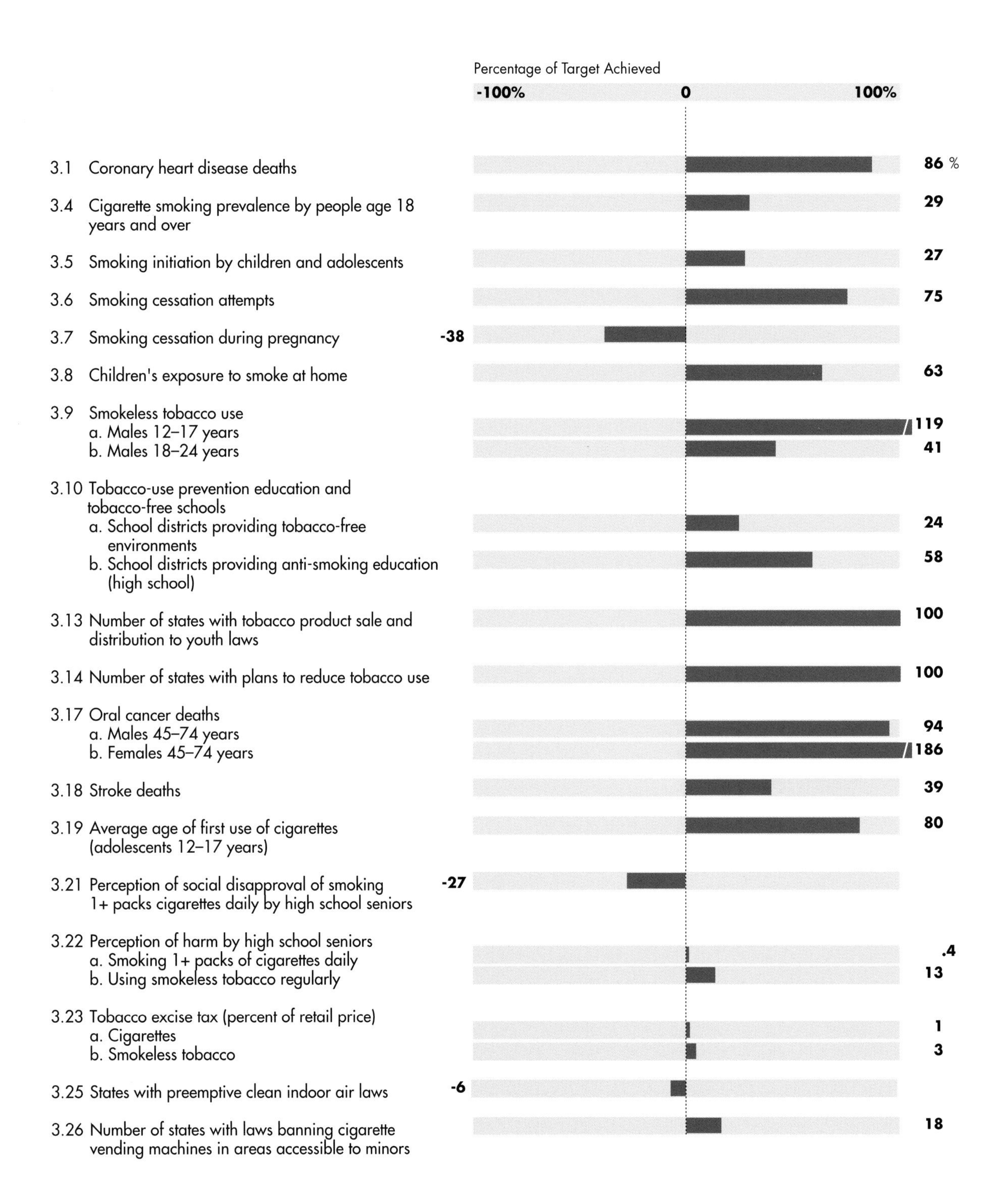

NOTES: The percentage of target achieved was not calculated for every tobacco-related objective. In 1990, the Department of Health and Human Services released its *Healthy People 2000* objectives, including those related to the use of tobacco, alcohol and other drugs, with the goal of improving the health of Americans by the end of the century. These charts report on the nation's progress toward these objectives, comparing baseline data from the 1990 report with the most recent data available by the end of 1999.

SOURCE: National Center for Health Statistics. *Healthy People 2000 Review, 1998–1999*. Hyattsville, MD: Public Health Service, 1999. Chart adapted by Brandeis staff.

Index

Note: Bold numbers refer to Indicator page numbers. Italicized page numbers refer to tables.

A

D

E

F

G

H

I

J

L

M

N

O

P

Q

R

S

V

W

Y